Jane Austen and the Military

Publisher
Website - www.BretwaldaBooks.com
Twitter - @Bretwaldabooks
Facebook - Bretwalda Books
Blog - bretwaldabooks.blogspot.co.uk/

Author:
Website - www.RupertMatthews.com;
Twitter - @HistoryRupert;
Facebook - @HistoryRupert

First Published 2017
Text Copyright © Rupert Matthews 2017
Photos and illustrations Copyright © Rupert Matthews 2017, unless otherwise stated
Rupert Matthews asserts his moral rights to be regarded as the author of this work. All rights reserved. No reproduction of any part of this publication is permitted without the prior written permission of the publisher:

ISBN 978-1-910440-49-0

The Front Cover shows [top] A portrait of Jane Austen. This late 19th century coloured engraving is based on a sketch of Austen completed by her sister Cassandra in about 1810. ; [bottom] The Battle of Quatre Bras, as painted by Lady Butler. This shows the British 28th Regiment of Foot being attacked by French cavalry at about 5pm on 16 June 1815. .

Contents

Introduction	The Napoleonic Wars	5
Chapter 1	Colonel Brandon and Foreign Service (Sense and Sensibility)	12
Chapter 2	George Wickham and the Militia (Pride & Prejudice)	27
Chapter 3	Colonel Fitzwilliam and the Purchase System (Pride & Prejudice)	39
Chapter 4	William Price and family influence (Mansfield Park)	53
Chapter 5	Mr Price and the Royal Marines (Mansfield Park)	70
Chapter 6	Mr Weston and Military Status (Emma)	77
Chapter 7	Frederick Wentworth and prize money (Persuasion)	86
Chapter 8	James Benwick and the Rating of Naval Ships (Persuasion)	107
Chapter 9	The Enigma of Admiral Croft (Persuasion)	115
Chapter 10	Conclusion	125

Jane Austen and the Military

Introduction
The Napoleonic Wars

Although Jane Austen wrote books about civilian life, manners and the role of women, the military loom large. Several characters are serving or former officers in the military and frequent reference is made to the army and the navy. This is hardly surprising. Austen lived in a world of war.

Born in 1775 and living until 1817, Jane Austen lived in a Britain at war for 32 of her 41 years. Compared to this astonishingly warlike period in British history, the world wars of the 20th century pale by comparison and the 21st Century is a haven of peace and tranquillity despite military campaigns in the Middle East.

Those wars had a massive influence on life in Britain. The French attempted to invade Britain more than once. In 1797, some 1,500 French troops landed at Fishguard in Wales. The Fishguard landing was intended by the French to act as a spark to raise a rebellion among the Welsh - who the revolutionary government in Paris fondly imagined to be oppressed Celtic peasants eager to rise in revolution against their English overlords. It turned out that the Welsh preferred not to join forces with the invaders. After a rather farcical two-day campaign, the French surrendered to the rapidly mustering Welsh militia at the Royal Oak pub.

The following year rather more success was gained in Ireland by two French landings in County Mayo and Donegal. The Irish were more inclined to rise than the Welsh. The 1798 Rising, led by Wolfe

Facing Page: A portrait of Jane Austen. This late 19th century coloured engraving is based on a sketch of Austen completed by her sister Cassandra in about 1810.

Jane Austen and the Military

Tone, eventually numbered around 50,000 rebels, backed by 5,000 French troops and 10 French warships. The British mustered 30,000 regulars, supported by some 70,000 armed loyal Irishmen. After six months of hard fighting, the rebellion was put down, though unrest continued to 1804.

The French, now under the control of the Emperor Napoleon, concluded that if Britain were to be invaded and knocked out of the war they would have to do the job properly. In the autumn of 1804, Napoleon began mustering a huge army in camps spread around Boulogne and Calais. Agents of the increasingly worried British government estimated that by March 1805 Napoleon had more than

A Martello Tower, dozens of which were built around the British coast to guard against a French invasion. When new the tower was topped by a large cannon mounted on a platform able to swivel round to fire in any direction. Infantry manned the outer wall as a defence against ground attack. Each tower had a permanent garrison of one officer and about 40 men. The design was taken from the fortress of Mortella in Corsica that put up a strong resistance to a British naval landing in 1794. [Photo: Stefan Flöper]

Jane Austen and the Military

200,000 men gathered ready to invade Britain. Vast numbers of barges and other craft were gathered in the Channel ports to carry the army across, and Napoleon even had dozens of hot air balloons - then the cutting edge of technology - ready to carry up scouts equipped with telescopes.

The British army was much smaller, so the defenders put their faith in static defences. Small forts, often dubbed Martello Towers, were built along the coast so that their guns could sweep any likely landing grounds with a hail of shot. The routes inland from the most likely landing spots were interrupted with water obstacles, and bridges over rivers or canals prepared for rapid demolition with gunpowder charges.

Above all the British relied on the Royal Navy to patrol the English Channel and stop the French invasion boats from crossing.

Napoleon was aware of the need to control the seas to get his army across safely. "Let us be masters of the Channel for six hours and we are masters of the world." he said in the spring of 1805. To achieve this, Napoleon planned for the Franco-Spanish fleets then in Toulon and Brest to put to sea. They were to head to Britain's economically important West Indies colonies. Once the British fleets headed across the Atlantic to protect their colonies, the Franco-Spanish ships were to dash back over the Atlantic, smash whatever British ships had been left in the Channel and so open the way for the invasion.

This was a time of real danger for Britain. If Napoleon had got even a fraction of his army over the narrow seas it is hard to imagine how Britain could have survived. Brave the militia may have been, but they were heavily outnumbered and lacked much in the way of equipment - most obviously artillery support.

The French army of 1805 was not noted for his good behaviour. Looting, rape and pillage were second nature to the French soldiers. Fired with revolutionary fervour, the French soldiers had torched manors and aristocratic houses the length of Europe.

Although Jane's family was relatively modest in terms of fortune,

Jane Austen and the Military

it was well connected and would undoubtedly have suffered as a result of an invasion by the French. Jane and her companions would have had a very real fear of rape. The fear of invasion reached a peak in the summer of 1805.

Then came news of the great naval battle of Trafalgar. The Franco-Spanish fleet had indeed put to sea, but it had been crushed by a fleet of the Royal Navy commanded by Admiral Lord Nelson. Of the 41 French and Spanish ships present at Trafalgar, no less than 21 were sunk or captured. The survivors headed for Cadiz. Two years later Spain changed sides, and all those ships that had escaped destruction come into British service.

When news of Trafalgar reached Britain, the sense of relief was immense. Invasion was no longer a realistic threat. Another ten years of war lay ahead, and much blood and money would be expended, but the prospect of utter defeat was removed. Jane and her family could rest easy in their beds.

It is therefore no wonder that Austen chose to include military characters in her novels. Most families of her class would have had relatives or friends serving in the military and would have expected any novel set in contemporary times to have included at least some reference to the on-going wars and to the military.

Not only that, but Austen's own brother was a serving officer in the Royal Navy. Charles Austen (1779-1852) joined the navy in 1791.

Charles Austen (1779-1852). Jane Austen's brother rose to be a Rear Admiral and died at sea at the age of 73 while still on active service. He married twice and produced seven children.

Jane Austen and the Military

By 1811, when Austen's first novel Sense and Sensibility, was published he had risen to the rank of Captain. When the book came out he commanded HMS Cleopatra, a 32-gun frigate, but within weeks he had shifted to HMS Namur, a much larger ship of the line with 74 guns. In this new command he was based at the Nore in the Thames Estuary and rarely put to sea, as his main task was to guard the access to London.

It was not until 1815 that Charles returned to an active command when he gained the 36-gun frigate HMS Phoenix. At first he blockaded Neapolitan warships in Brindisi - Naples then being an ally of France. When peace came Charles turned to hunting pirates in the eastern Mediterranean, capturing two pirate ships near Pavos.

In February 1816, the Phoenix was guided on to rocks off Smyrna by her pilots and totally wrecked. Charles managed to get his entire crew ashore by using the fallen mizzen mast as a bridge to scramble over to the shore. Charles sold the wreck to a local scrap merchant before hiring a merchant ship to take him and his crew to Malta where he reported the loss of his ship. Losing a ship under any circumstances was a serious matter in the Royal Navy, so Charles found himself in front of a court martial. He was absolved of any blame and returned to the active list, though by then Jane has passed away. Charles went on to some fame and fortune attaining the rank of Rear Admiral before his death.

Sir Francis Austen (1774-1865) was Jane's other brother in the Royal Navy. After an adventurous career at sea, which can be seen to have inspired several naval characters in Jane's novels, he finally reached the pinnacle of his career on 27 April 1863 when he became the Admiral of the Fleet - the most senior position in the Royal Navy.

Jane Austen and the Military

As we shall see, Jane almost certainly used her brother's career as source material in her novels. But he was not her only relative to see military service. Another brother, Francis Austen (1774-1865) also joined the Royal Navy. His career was more adventurous than that of Charles. After 13 years as a junior officer, he gained his first command in 1799. With the sloop HMS Peterel, Francis roved the Mediterranean, capturing some 40 French merchant ships and taking a French naval brig off Marseilles.

In 1801 he was given command of the brand new HMS Neptune, a prestigious command as it was a line of battle of ship mounting 98 guns. He only narrowly missed fighting at the Battle of Trafalgar in 1805. His absence was due to the fact that he was escorting a vital convoy of merchant ships at the time.

By 1808 he commanded the ancient 64 gun ship HMS St Albans. In this ship he escorted the convoy carrying a British army to Portugal under Sir Arthur Wellesley [later to gain fame as the Duke of Wellington]. From the deck of this ship Francis watched Wellesley defeat the French at the Battle of Vimeiro.

After three years of quiet service in the North Sea, Francis took a new ship, the 120 gun HMS Caledonia, across the Atlantic to fight the Americans in the War of 1812. He launched a successful campaign against American privateers, securing the seas for British merchant ships. By the time of Jane's death Francis had been made a Companion of the Order of the Bath. He later rose to be Admiral of the Fleet - the highest rank in the Royal Navy - and was knighted.

Jane's other brother to see military service was Henry (1771-1850). Today he is best known today as the clergyman who arranged for the posthumous publication of Northanger Abbey and Persuasion. But Henry did not enter the Church until 1816, after his earlier career in banking ended ignominiously in bankruptcy.

As a younger man Henry had been a rather dashing fellow. He studied at St John's College, Oxford, and gained an MA in 1793. That same year he joined the Oxfordshire Militia as an officer and rose to

Jane Austen and the Military

the rank of Captain by the time he resigned his commission to enter the world of banking. No doubt Henry gave Jane much material that she could use in forming her characters who served in the militia.

Although neither of Jane's other brothers saw service, these three gave her plenty of material with which to work. They also demonstrate that the military were a far more prominent presence in the life of a middle class girl in Austen's day than they would be today.

It was, therefore, only natural for Jane to include military characters in her writing. But given that she herself had never seen service and that her focus was always on the female characters, the question must arise as to just how accurate her writings about the military were.

To discover the accuracy, or otherwise, of Jane Austen's representations of the military it is best to look at what she says about the best known military men in her novels.

"Scotland Forever", a painting by Lady Butler that shows the charge of the Scots Greys at the Battle of Waterloo in 1815. The defeat of the French Emperor Napoleon at Waterloo by the British Duke of Wellington effectively marked the end of the wars that had shaken Europe since 1793.

 *Jane Austen and the Military*

Chapter 1

Colonel Brandon and Foreign Service

(Sense and Sensibility)

The novel Sense and Sensibility was published in 1811, and was the first of Jane Austen's novels to go into print - though Northanger Abbey was the first to be written. Unlike most of her novels, which were set loosely in the present day, Sense and Sensibility was set in the very specific date range of 1792 to 1797.

The military figure in the novel is Colonel Brandon - a major character and love interest - whose army days are behind him when the novel opens. When he is first introduced to us in Chapter 7, Austen makes very clear that he is a military man for the first word she writes is "Colonel". We meet him when the two younger Dashwood sisters - Marianne and Margaret - go to visit their benefactor Sir John Middleton and his family. Sir John explains that he has a friend visiting. After describing Sir John's wife and mother-in-law Austen turns to this friend.

The paragraph runs like this:

"Colonel Brandon, the friend of Sir John, seemed no more adapted by resemblance of manner to be his friend, than Lady Middleton was to be his wife, or Mrs. Jennings to be Lady Middleton's mother. He was silent and grave. His appearance however was not unpleasing, in spite of his being in the opinion of Marianne and Margaret an absolute old bachelor, for he was on the wrong side of five and thirty; but

Jane Austen and the Military

though his face was not handsome, his countenance was sensible, and his address was particularly gentlemanlike."

At this point we learn nothing about his military career other than that he holds the rank of Colonel and that he is, apparently, not on active service. Although not much, this does allow us to make a number of deductions about Colonel Brandon and his career to date.

First of all his age of "the wrong side of five and thirty" is about right for a youngish colonel. Of course this phrase could mean any age over 35, but if he had been 39 then surely Austen would have written "nearly forty". We can assume that he is 36 or maybe 37, but

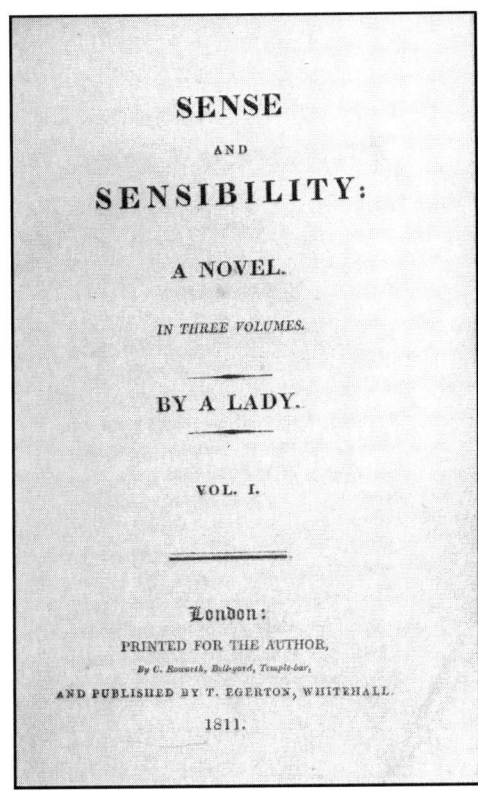

The title page of the first edition of Sense and Sensibility. *Jane Austen's name is not mentioned and she is described only as being "a lady", a description which gave her readers a clear idea of her social standing but no idea of her identity.*

Jane Austen and the Military

not much older. Brandon is, therefore, some years older than Colonel Fitzwilliam of Pride and Prejudice. Even so, being a colonel at the age of 35 would imply that his family had purchased at least some of his promotions for him. Nobody relying on talent, luck and non-purchase commissions could reasonably hope to reach the rank of colonel by the age of 35.

We will return the purchase of army commissions in more detail when considering Colonel Fitzwilliam, but for now it is enough to remark that it was possible to purchase a number of ranks in the army, but that it was fiendishly expensive to do so. Austen's readers would have known and appreciated this without being told. It is, therefore, an early hint of the fact that Colonel Brandon is a gentleman of some wealth. In the context of Austen's main focus on the impoverished Dashwood girls this makes him a likely good prospect as a marriage partner.

That said, the financial aspect of his character remains rather mysterious for some time. In Chapter 14, Mrs Jennings says of him "I am afraid his circumstances may be bad. The estate at Delaford was never reckoned more than two thousand a year, and his brother left everything sadly involved."

Now, £2,000 per year would have been a substantial income at this date, equivalent to perhaps £2 million today. In Austen's world this is thought pretty good, though not as handsome as the £10,000 a year produced by the estate of Mr Darcy in Pride and Prejudice. However, as Mrs Jennings says, the estate was "sadly involved". This could mean a number of things in the early 19th century but basically it meant that Brandon was a lot poorer than he might appear.

It might be that Brandon's elder brother had borrowed large sums of money, using the estate as collateral. In this case, Brandon would be paying the money back, rather like a modern mortgage, out of the income generated by the estate. In that case he would have a disposable income much less than the claimed £2,000. On the other hand, the elder brother may have borrowed cash and signed over the

Jane Austen and the Military

rent from farms and other properties on the estate for a set number of years to repay the lender. This would mean that Brandon never sees the money in the first place. It goes straight to the lender. Mrs Jenning's words would seem to imply that the latter was the case.

In Chapter 34, Brandon tells Elinor Dashwood something more about Delaford. In the course of a long conversation about the younger Eliza - the illegitimate daughter of the older Eliza with whom Brandon had been in love as a young man - the colonel says:

"I saw her there whenever I could, and after the death of my brother, (which happened about five years ago, and which left to me the possession of the family property,) she visited me at Delaford."

So far as the novel is concerned the main point of the conversation is to give us more information about Eliza, and at the same time to show Brandon as being a generous and warm hearted guardian. However, it is made very clear that during the intervening five years since his brother's death, Colonel Brandon has been based at Delaford. In other words, he was not with his regiment. That would mean that he had attained the rank of colonel by about the age of 30. As with Colonel Fitzwilliam in Pride and Prejudice this puts him firmly in the ranks of the wealthy elite who had purchased their promotions. We can't help wondering how a family encumbered with huge debts could afford to do this.

We get our next, and most important, bit of information about Colonel Brandon's military career in Chapter 34 when he is talking to Elinor about his long lost love, the elder Eliza, and about his feelings towards Marianne. It is a long speech for one of Austen's novels, and a very long monologue for Brandon. He says of Eliza:

"This lady was one of my nearest relations, an orphan from her infancy, and under the guardianship of my father. Our ages were nearly the same, and from our earliest years we were playfellows and friends. I cannot remember the time when I did not love Eliza; and my affection for her, as we grew up, was

such, as perhaps, judging from my present forlorn and cheerless gravity, you might think me incapable of having ever felt. Hers, for me, was, I believe, fervent as the attachment of your sister to Mr. Willoughby and it was, though from a different cause, no less unfortunate. At seventeen she was lost to me for ever. She was married—married against her inclination to my brother. Her fortune was large, and our family estate much encumbered. And this, I fear, is all that can be said for the conduct of one, who was at once her uncle and guardian. My brother did not deserve her; he did not even love her. I had hoped that her regard for me would support her under any difficulty, and for some time it did; but at last the misery of her situation, for she experienced "great unkindness, overcame all her resolution, and though she had promised me that nothing—but how blindly I relate! I have never told you how this was brought on. We were within a few hours of eloping together for Scotland. The treachery, or the folly, of my cousin's maid betrayed us. I was banished to the house of a relation far distant, and she was allowed no liberty, no society, no amusement, till my father's point was gained. I had depended on her fortitude too far, and the blow was a severe one—but had her marriage been happy, so young as I then was, a few months must have reconciled me to it, or at least I should not have now to lament it. This however was not the case. My brother had no regard for her; his pleasures were not what they ought to have been, and from the first he treated her unkindly. The consequence of this, upon a mind so young, so lively, so inexperienced as Mrs. Brandon's, was but too natural. She resigned herself at first to all the misery of her situation; and happy had it been if she had not lived to overcome "those regrets which the remembrance of me occasioned. But can we wonder that, with such a husband to provoke inconstancy, and without a friend to advise or restrain her (for my father lived

Jane Austen and the Military

only a few months after their marriage, and I was with my regiment in the East Indies) she should fall? Had I remained in England, perhaps—but I meant to promote the happiness of both by removing from her for years, and for that purpose had procured my exchange. The shock which her marriage had given me," he continued, in a voice of great agitation, *"was of trifling weight—was nothing to what I felt when I heard, about two years afterwards, of her divorce."*

After taking a break to recover from the distress caused by speaking of these events, Colonel Brandon continues:

""It was nearly three years after this unhappy period before I returned to England. My first care, when I DID arrive, was of course to seek for her; but the search was as fruitless as it was melancholy. I could not trace her beyond her first seducer, and there was every reason to fear that she had removed from him only to sink deeper in a life of sin. Her legal allowance was not adequate to her fortune, nor sufficient for her comfortable maintenance, and I learnt from my brother that the power of receiving it had been made over some months before to another person. He imagined, and calmly could he imagine it, that her extravagance, and consequent distress, had obliged her to dispose of it for some immediate relief. At last, however, and after I had been six months in England, I DID find her."

It transpires that Eliza was already dying of consumption [today we would all it tuberculosis] leaving behind a baby girl, also called Eliza. This baby is taken on by Colonel Brandon as his ward - though it leads local gossips to assume it is his illegitimate child.

Leaving aside the complexities of the plot, this long speech by Colonel Brandon tells us pretty much all we know about his military career. Putting together what he does tell us we learn the following. At the time of the planned, but failed, elopement the elder Eliza was aged 17 and Brandon was of a similar age. At first Brandon was then

Jane Austen and the Military

"banished to the house of a relation far distant" for an unspecified period of time until Eliza had agreed to marry Brandon's elder brother.

Brandon then decided to go abroad because as he says "I meant to promote the happiness of both by removing from her for years, and for that purpose had procured my exchange". This is a key point that contemporaries of Austen would have fully understood.

Within the system of purchasing commissions within the army, it was possible for an officer to swap - or exchange - his commission with another officer of the same rank in a different regiment. This involved no payment to the government and was, in theory at least, a straight swap between the two officers concerned. The permission of the colonels of the two regiments was required, but otherwise it was a private matter. It was not, however, one that did not have its cost.

The officers in the army were a fairly mixed bunch. Some had money, some did not. Some had a social status to maintain, others did not. A few had political ambitions, most did not. Some saw the army as a life long career, others viewed it as a way to gain social prestige before going home to run the family estates. This mixture meant that different officers preferred different regiments, different postings and different experiences.

What Brandon says that he did was to exchange his commission in a regiment posted in Britain with another officer who was in a regiment stationed in the East Indies. As a general rule, it was the richer officers, or those with social or political ambitions who preferred to be stationed in Britain. Poorer officers or those viewing the army as a career preferred the more distant stations where there was more likely to be fighting - and therefore the chance to win glory. This meant that the sort of exchange that Brandon is talking about would normally see the officer moving to the regiment in Britain pay a hefty bounty to the officer taking his place in distant lands.

Brandon does not say that he took such a cash payment in return for his exchange, but those reading Austen's book when it first came out would surely have assumed that he did. This assumption would

Jane Austen and the Military

be all the more natural given that we know that Delaford, Brandon's estate, was in hock for a considerable amount of debt.

It is here that we run into something of a problem with Brandon's military career. Given that he is aged about 36 or 37 at the time he is speaking and that he was about 18 when Eliza got married this would mean that he was aged perhaps 20 when he exchanged his commission and headed to the East Indies. Given that the book is set in the mid-1790s, that means that he left England in around 1775 or thereabouts. And that makes no real sense in relation to Britain's involvement in the East Indies.

At this date the "East Indies" was a rather vague geographical term. It referred loosely to those assorted lands that lay east of India but south of China and north of Australia. The boundaries were never clearly defined, but would have included the modern states of Thailand, Malaysia, Laos, Vietnam, Indonesia, Cambodia, Brunei and Singapore. Some people might have included what is now Burma

The settlement of Penang at the time that the British first opened a trading post there Despite the presence of the British East India Company in the area there was no British army unit in the area for some years to follow.

Jane Austen and the Military

[Myanmar] in the East Indies, others might have felt it fell under the term "India". Similarly New Guinea, Timor and adjacent islands may be been thought of in the East Indies, or as part of Australia.

At time that Sense and Sensibility was published, the British had several trading posts in this area. Penang and Perai had been important ports in the hands of the British for some years along with smaller places in the Malay Peninsula. Indeed, at the time Austen published this book the East Indies was the scene of a good deal of military action for the British. The origins of that involvement lay in the Netherlands.

In 1801 a French-backed coup d'etat took place in the Netherlands that threw out the old regime and installed a revolutionary government backed by the army. At this date the Netherlands had a substantial empire in the East Indies. They did not actually own all that much territory, but they did own several important ports of which the largest were Malacca and Amboina, plus several in Sumatra. The Dutch had also negotiated exclusive trade deals with several rulers in the East Indies. This gave the Dutch a lucrative monopoly on trade between the East Indies and Europe, in return for which they paid a cash sum each year to the local rulers. When the coup took place those colonies and important trade deals fell to the pro-French government in the Netherlands.

Then, in 1806, Napoleon tired of acting through his puppet government in the Hague. French troops marched into the Netherlands, overthrew the new revolutionary government and seized control of key fortresses, ports and government buildings. The occupiers then proclaimed that the Netherlands was now a kingdom for the first time in its history. The new king who moved quickly to occupy the new throne was a man by the name of Louis Bonaparte, who just happened to be Napoleon's younger brother.

The more extreme revolutionaries welcomed the move as they believed that it would entrench the social and legal changes that had been sparked by the French revolution. More patriotic or reactionary

Jane Austen and the Military

Dutch folk were less certain. In the colonies the Dutch authorities feared that they were about to be invaded and annexed by France.

This was no empty fear. Fleets of French warships were at large in the Indian and Pacific Oceans, plundering and pillaging enemy merchant ships. And Napoleon had a track record of stripping the assets of the countries he conquered to fill the coffers of the French government. The Dutch authorities and merchants had good reason to believe that they wealth, position and possibly their lives would all be lost of they submitted to the government of the new King Louis.

The Dutch colonial authorities decided that instead they would declare their loyalty to the ousted old regime, and ask Britain for military protection. Britain was only too happy to provide naval and military support in return for a cut of the highly lucrative Dutch monopolies. The local authorities and merchants were left alone, but the trade back to Europe was no carried out by British ships sailing to British ports.

British troops were shipped in to garrison the Dutch possessions to protect them against any French invasion. The lands to which they went were hot, disease-ridden and many months sailing time away from Britain. This combination of factors made the postings enormously unpopular with socially ambitious or wealthy officers. Such men in regiments earmarked for the East Indies would have eagerly exchanged their commissions with poorer officers in regiments staying Europe - and would have paid a hefty fee for doing so. Austen and her readers would have known all this when Sense and Sensibility was published in 1811. Brandon's account of his own exchange would therefore have been entirely credible and would have been exactly the sort of thing that an officer who wanted to get out of England for some years would have done - and made a good profit at the same time.

Unfortunately, Britain's occupation of the Dutch colonies did not start until 1806. The earlier establishment of the much smaller scale British colonies at Penang and Perai had begun in 1791. And yet the

Jane Austen and the Military

dating of events in Sense and Sensibility means that Brandon left to join a British regiment going to the East Indies in the mid to late 1770s.

There were, quite simply, no British garrisons in the East Indies at that date. Brandon could not, therefore, have been "with my

An early 19th century duel. In this illustration the artist has put the two duellists closer together than they would have been in real life. A distance of about 20 paces or so was usual, which given the poor accuracy of pistols at this date made for a higher rater of survival among participants than might otherwise be expected.

Jane Austen and the Military

regiment in the East Indies". It is a clear mistake on the part of Jane Austen. She was thinking of and writing about the conditions of the time when she was writing, not those of the past when Brandon had been a young man.

We should then turn to perhaps the most dramatic moment in Brandon's career - though it takes place off stage as it were and we only learn about it second hand. This comes when he fights a duel with Willoughby, the rakish young man who seduced and got pregnant Eliza the younger, Brandon's ward. We learn of this duel in Chapter 31 during a conversation between Brandon and Elinor. Brandon first explains how Willoughby had behaved, and his own fears for the fate of Marianne should she continue to see Willoughby. There then follows this exchange, with Elinor speaking first:

"I have been more pained," said she, "by her endeavours to acquit him than by all the rest; for it irritates her mind more than the most perfect conviction of his unworthiness can do. Now, though at first she will suffer much, I am sure she will soon become easier. Have you," she continued, after a short silence, "ever seen Mr. Willoughby since you left him at Barton?"

"Yes," he replied gravely, "once I have. One meeting was unavoidable."

Elinor, startled by his manner, looked at him anxiously, saying,

"What? have you met him to—"

"I could meet him no other way. Eliza had confessed to me, though most reluctantly, the name of her lover; and when he returned to town, which was within a fortnight after myself, we met by appointment, he to defend, I to punish his conduct. We returned unwounded, and the meeting, therefore, never got abroad."

Elinor sighed over the fancied necessity of this; but to a man and a soldier she presumed not to censure it.

Jane Austen and the Military

This is an interesting exchange. Austen does not use the word "duel", though this is clearly what she means. Instead she uses the euphemism "meeting", which was quite a common term at the time.

It must be assumed from what he says that Brandon had challenged Willoughby to a duel. At this date nearly all duels in England were fought with pistols. When a challenge was made, the first action taken by the participants was to choose what was known as a "second". This was a man who would act for him in the preparation for the duel. First the seconds would seek to avoid the duel taking place at all. Insults thrown when men had been drinking were often regretted next day and a swift apology would be made.

In this case, of course, no apology could avoid the duel. The seconds would therefore arrange a time and place for the duel, and prepare the weapons. Typically these would be a pair of identical pistols. The seconds would carefully weigh out the powder and inspect the bullets, then load both pistols carefully to ensure that both were as identical as possible. The man who had been challenged then had the choice of which pistol to take with the challenger being given the other one.

Each man would take up a position previously agreed by the seconds. Typically the "stands" would be about 20 to 30 yards apart. Given the inaccuracy of the smooth bore, short barrelled pistols of the time there was a pretty fair chance that not even a good shot would hit a man at this distance. Depending on what the seconds had agreed it might be that both men fired at the same time, or that one fired first.

Very often a duel was considered to be an affair of honour, not one of revenge. In this instance the men might deliberately miss each other. It was enough to satisfy their honour that the two men had faced each other with loaded weapons and risked death. In 1829, for instance, the Duke of Wellington fought a duel with the Earl of Winchelsea. Wellington fired first, and missed. Opinion differed as to whether he had deliberately missed or not, though given he was considered a good shot it is likely his miss was deliberate. Winchelsea

Jane Austen and the Military

then fired his pistol into the air. The seconds then held a discussion, after which Winchelsea rode home. He sat down and wrote a fulsome apology for the words he had said and sent the letter to a newspaper so that it could be publicly published.

Usually the duel was over when both men had fired their pistols. If one or the other were wounded, a doctor was usually on hand to minister to the wounds. Fatalities were rather rare at this date, but they did take place.

By this date duelling in Britain was increasingly frowned upon socially and was condemned outright by the Church but the legal position was far from clear. Fighting a duel was not illegal, although trying to kill another person was. A man who killed another in a duel was, in law, guilty of murder. However, juries were often reluctant to convict a man of murder after a duel. If the defendant could show that the duel had been conducted properly, fairly and in accordance with the dictates of honour then a jury was likely to find him not guilty. Even when a guilty verdict was handed down, the jury often added a plea for clemency and judges did not impose the death penalty.

So when Brandon says "the meeting, therefore, never got abroad" he means that there were non-legal repercussions.

There was, however, one circumstance in which the law on duelling was rigorously enforced. It was absolutely illegal for military officers to fight duels. It must be remembered that Britain was fighting a war against France and her allies that dragged on for decades. The country simply could not afford to lose talented military officers to duels over affairs of honour. Willoughby may not have been an army officer, but Colonel Brandon certainly was. If news of his "meeting" with Willoughby had "got abroad" he - and everyone else involved - would have been in very serious trouble indeed.

That there is no hint of this in Sense and Sensibility raises another question mark over Brandon's military career. For a military man of relatively high rank during a war, he spends a huge amount of time at home or visiting his social friends and, indeed, courting Marianne

Jane Austen and the Military

Dashwood. That raises the question of whether Colonel Brandon is actually still a colonel at the time the events of the novel unfold.

It was perfectly possible for an officer to resign his commission in the army, providing he got permission to do so from the monarch - in practice the commander in chief. Having obtained such permission, the officer could put his commission up for purchase. The transaction would have to be approved, of course, but in this way an officer could get a nice cash payment to help him in his retirement. We know that Brandon is short of cash, albeit that he owns a valuable estate. Selling his commission and retiring from the army would be a perfectly natural thing for a man in his position to do. Noticeably, however, Austen does not say whether or not Brandon has done this. It might be a natural assumption for a reader in 1811 to make, but there is no conclusive proof that Brandon had done so.

In conclusion, it is clear that in handling Brandon's military career, Jane Austen did not do a very good job.

First, he seems to have managed to get to the rank of Colonel at a young age. This must mean that he had access to large sums of money to purchase his commissions - yet Austen makes it very clear that the family is short of money and deep in debt.

Second, Brandon fought a duel when it was illegal for him to do so, but nobody comments on the fact and Elinor accepts his actions quite calmly.

Third, and most seriously, Austen has him going to the East Indies with his regiment some 10 years or so before any British troops were stationed there at all.

Sense and Sensibility is a great novel, and Brandon is a believable and popular character. It is unfortunate, therefore, that in her first effort to deal with military Austen made such errors with his military career. Would she do any better in her next novel: *Pride and Prejudice?*

Chapter 2
George Wickham and the Militia

(Pride & Prejudice)

Our first military man in Jane Austen's works perhaps the best known and - at least in the books - the most militarily active. George Wickham is a great character. Outwardly he is charming, respectable and honest, he is later revealed to be a cad and a bounder of the very worst kind. He is a key character in the unfolding plot of Pride and Prejudice, but it is his military career that is of interest to us here.

When Wickham first appears he has only just joined the military. He is introduced to us thus:

"But the attention of every lady was soon caught by a young man, whom they had never seen before, of most gentlemanlike appearance, walking with another officer on the other side of the way. The officer was the very Mr. Denny concerning whose return from London Lydia came to inquire, and he bowed as they passed. All were struck with the stranger's air, all wondered who he could be; and Kitty and Lydia, determined if possible to find out, led the way across the street, under pretence of wanting something in an opposite shop, and fortunately had just gained the pavement when the two gentlemen, turning back, had reached the same spot. Mr. Denny addressed them directly, and entreated permission to introduce his friend, Mr. Wickham, who had returned with him the day

Jane Austen and the Military

before from town, and he was happy to say had accepted a commission in their corps. This was exactly as it should be; for the young man wanted only regimentals to make him completely charming. His appearance was greatly in his favour; he had all the best part of beauty, a fine countenance, a good figure, and very pleasing address. The introduction was followed up on his side by a happy readiness of conversation— a readiness at the same time perfectly correct and unassuming: and the whole party were still standing and talking together very agreeably, when the sound of horses drew their notice, and Darcy and Bingley were seen riding down the street."

Here Jane Austen is showing us Wickham as he appeared to Kitty and Lydia. He is superficially charming and proper. The military intrude only to provide a reason for him being in Meryton and to give us the information that he wanted only to get on a uniform to make his appearance perfect.

The "corps" referred to here had been introduced to the reader some pages earlier. We first learn of this when Lydia and Kitty visit their aunt, Mrs Philips, in Meryton. The unit in question is described as being "a militia regiment" which is going into winter quarters and will remain the whole winter. In the book Jane Austen gives no further details for the very good reason that her readers would have known exactly what she meant.

The book was first published in 1813, at a time when there were some 80,000 men under arms in the militia. The British militia had existed for centuries, and was of rather variable quality. But by the time of Pride and Prejudice the threat of French invasion and vigorous government action had made the militia into a disciplined and effective military force.

Each county had to raise a regiment of militia, in theory comprising 800 men. Every able-bodied man in the county aged between 18 and 50 had to register for the militia. A ballot was then held with the names of 800 men to serve in the militia chosen at

Jane Austen and the Military

random. Any man who did not want to serve could avoid service either by paying a fee of £10 or by persuading somebody else to take his place. In peacetime this inevitably meant that the ranks of the militia were made up of the poorest men in the county. Either they could not afford the £10 to evade duty or they had been paid by a more wealthy neighbour to sign up in their place.

Once in the militia, each man was given a uniform, musket, bayonet and other equipment. It was his responsibility to care for these and heavy fines were imposed for lost or damaged equipment. Militia uniforms were very similar to those of the regular army with red coats

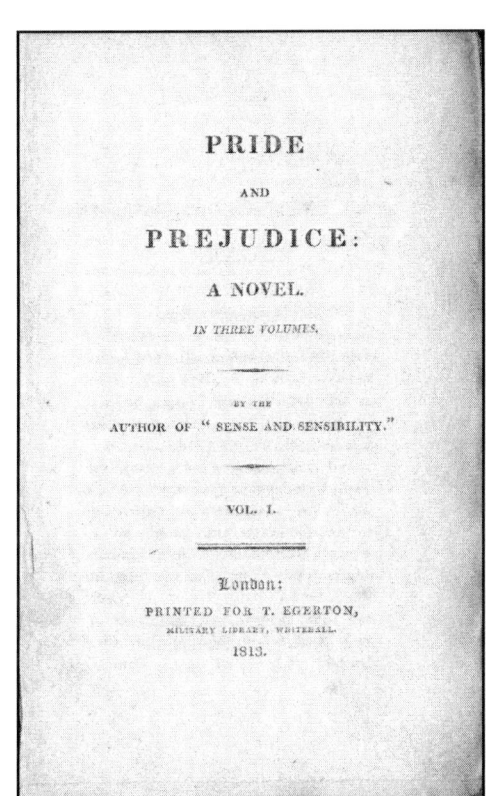

The title page of the original edition of Pride and Prejudice. Once again, Jane Austen is not mentioned by name although she is identified as the author of Sense and Sensibility in an effort to build up a loyal following of readers.

Jane Austen and the Military

paired to grey or white trousers and a tall black hat known as a shako. Details such as the design of the buttons and colour of the cuffs and collars distinguished the militia units from the regular army and from each other.

Once recruited, a militia regiment was expected to form up for about one month each summer for training. The regiment would march away from its home county - largely so that nobody was tempted to slip home for dinner - and camped out in the open fields. Often several regiments were brought together to practice more complex co-operation and battlefield manoeuvres. While the militia

An officer in the militia, in this case the Norfolk Militia. Although each militia unit was free to choose details about its uniform, they all had to conform to a national patter regarding colour, cut and style. Wickham would have been dressed in a uniform similar to this.

Jane Austen and the Military

regiment were "embodied", as it was known, the men were paid the same as those in the regular army: one shilling per day, the famous "King's Shilling". By the time of Pride and Prejudice, the militia were "embodied" permanently rather than for just a few weeks each summer.

The officers of the militia were all volunteers. Like the men, were paid on a par with the regular army officers. On joining up with the rank of Lieutenant, Wickham would have been paid around £100 per year. Given that the average working man would be lucky to get £20 a year at this date that was not a bad rate of pay. Indeed, we later learn that the prospect of pay was one of the reasons why the spendthrift Wickham volunteered.

Alongside the militia were the Yeomanry. These units do not feature in Pride and Prejudice, but would probably have loomed larger in rural society than the militia in most counties. While the militia were infantry serving for pay and recruited by a form of conscription, the yeomanry were cavalry volunteers who brought their own equipment to the job. This inevitably meant that the only men able to serve in the yeomanry were those who owned their own horse and could afford the not inconsiderable cost of uniform, weapons and supplies. Yeomanry officers were drawn from the nobility and gentry - their bills being considerably higher than those of the rank and file.

Yeomanry regiments were famous for their flamboyant uniforms, lively social calendars and socially elevated membership. It is probably for this reason that Jane chose to put Wickham into a militia regiment rather than a Yeomanry unit. While a Yeomanry unit arriving in Meryton would have made a much greater splash among the local residents, and the officers would have been more attractive to the young ladies, the impoverished Wickham would never have been able to afford the costs of being a yeomanry officer. It is also likely that Darcy would have quickly heard of Wickham joining a yeomanry unit and, given his own socially elevated status, have been able to get him thrown out fairly quickly.

Jane Austen and the Military

When the militia appear in Meryton they are going into winter quarters. This was made necessary by the weather. At this date soldiering was generally a summer profession. Sleeping out in the open, even in tents, would render men unfit for fighting or marching fairly quickly between October and March. Instead the regiment would be marched to a town where men and officers could find snug indoor quarters in pubs, private houses, barns and outhouses. The officers, with rather more money to spend, got the best quarters while the men slept where they were put. During the winter the regiment would be kept fairly busy drilling and maintaining their equipment, but even so they would have had plenty of spare time on their hands - which is how Wickham has plenty of time to ingratiate himself with local society, and to woo first Mary King and then Lydia.

Indeed, as the novel unfolds it becomes clear that Wickham is using the social status that he has acquired as an officer in the militia to indulge his less reputable habits. We are not told that he had gone so far as to seduce any of the local young women, though it is hinted at.

When Wickham's commanding officer, Colonel Forster, belatedly comes to realise the lieutenant's true character he remarks in Chapter 45 that Wickham had been "imprudent". This can be taken to mean that Wickham had indulged in flirtations and romances, though it need not mean anything more serious.

More serious is the remark in Chapter 48 that *"He was declared to be in debt to every tradesman in the place, and his intrigues, all honoured with the title of seduction, had been extended into every tradesman's family."* Again the word "intrigue" carried a similar meaning at this date to that of "imprudent" - a love affair, with clear overtones of something improper or disreputable.

To modern ears the word "seduction" would clearly mean a sexual relationship, but again this was not quite so clear in the early 19th century. "To persuade or cause someone to do something that they would not usually consider doing by being very attractive and difficult

Jane Austen and the Military

to refuse," would be a perfectly normal meaning of the word in Austen's day.

Given that Wickham was intent on marrying Mary King and her £10,000 it would have been very foolish of him to get any other woman into bed, no matter how willing she would have been to give in to his charms.

In any case, the same extract is rather more definite about Wickham's other sin - excessively extravagant spending. In Chapter 45, when Elizabeth is at Pemberton, she is told that in earlier days Wickham *"had left many debts behind him, which Mr. Darcy afterwards discharged."*

In Chapter 49 we learn that when Wickham *"had left gaming debts behind him to a very considerable amount. Colonel Forster believed that more than a thousand pounds would be necessary to clear his expenses at Brighton. He owed a good deal in town, but his debts of honour were still more formidable."*

The scale of Wickham's debts appear to become a little clearer in Chapter 50 when Mr Gardiner catches up with him and Lydia. He states that £1,000 will clear all of Wickham's debts and that a settlement of £100 a year will keep them well provided for. Mr Bennett, however, does not believe this. He reckons that Wickham could quite easily demand £10,000 as the price for marrying Lydia and making an honest woman of her. They suspect that Mr Gardiner - Mrs Bennett's brother - has put up the money since he has been conducting the negotiations with Wickham.

It later transpires, in Chapter 53, that it was Mr Darcy who had found Wickham and Lydia and who had put up the money. Darcy had gone further, as we learn a few pages later, as Elizabeth reads in a letter from her uncle, Mr Gardiner:

"You know pretty well, I suppose, what has been done for the young people. His debts are to be paid, amounting, I believe, to considerably more than a thousand pounds, another thousand in addition to her own settled upon her, and his

Jane Austen and the Military

commission purchased. The reason why all this was to be done by him alone, was such as I have given above. It was owing to him, to his reserve and want of proper consideration, that Wickham's character had been so misunderstood, and consequently that he had been received and noticed as he was. Perhaps there was some truth in this; though I doubt whether his reserve, or anybody's reserve, can be answerable for the event. But in spite of all this fine talking, my dear Lizzy, you may rest perfectly assured that your uncle would never have yielded, if we had not given him credit for another interest in the affair."

We will return to this matter of "his commission purchased" in a later chapter, but for now it is enough to note that this means that Darcy expended a fair amount of money getting Wickham a commission as an officer in the regular army.

That the shopkeepers, pub landlords and tradesmen of Meryton had offered easy terms of debt to Wickham was perfectly understandable. For a start, this sort of debt was perfectly normal at this date.

Gentry did not carry money around with them. Instead they had accounts at all the local shops and other businesses. Whenever they ordered something or went shopping, the amount they spent was added to their bill. Those bills were due to be paid on what were known as the "quarter days", which were:

Lady Day (25 March)
Midsummer Day (24 June)
Michaelmas (29 September)
Christmas (25 December).

In the sort of small community that Meryton appears to be, these quarter days were very important. All sorts of bills were paid - including rents and household bills. Not only that but servants, farm hands and workshop workers were hired from one quarter day to the next. Although it is not mentioned in Pride and Prejudice, it was not

Jane Austen and the Military

uncommon for fairs or special markets to be held on these all important quarter days.

It was quite normal for an officer such as Wickham to ask to open an account at shops or businesses where he was going to be resident for some time. Everybody knew that the militia regiment was going to stay in Meryton until the spring. It would be natural for the officers to open accounts and promise to settle them at Christmas and then again on Lady Day. Wickham got past Christmas without trouble, but he left Meryton in early May. We know that he left behind him huge debts. It would have been difficult for him to rack up massive debts between the end of March and start of May, so presumably he had not settled his accounts on Lady Day but instead had allowed them to roll over. No doubt he had used his charm and easy way of telling lies to fob off the shop owners.

That they allowed themselves to be duped was down to their perception of Wickham. He had appeared in the guise of an officer of militia and was, therefore, quite clearly a gentleman of some means. Hertfordshire, where the novel is set, is about 130 miles from Derbyshire, where Wickham is from. That is quite a distance today, but in 1813 it would have been a very great distance indeed. Few people would have travelled such a distance regularly and certainly none of the tradesmen would have been to Derbyshire much. They would not have had contacts in Derbyshire and so could not check out Wickham as they would normally have done. His status as a militia officer was what they had to go on and, usually, that would have been enough.

The vast majority of officers in a county militia were, like the men, from the county. They would all have come from the fairly small circle of gentry families in that county. They would have known each other for years, would have known each other's ancestry, relatives and financial status. No man would have been accepted into a militia unit as an officer unless his county friends and acquaintances were confident that he would make a congenial comrade in arms.

Jane Austen and the Military

However, as readers of the book we know that Wickham had joined the regiment only once it arrived in Meryton and not when it had been in its native county. He was, therefore, not known to the militia's officers as a neighbour and friend. Instead he was brought into the regiment by Denny, who had only recently met him.

The circumstances under which Wickham joined the regiment are rather obscure. It is said that Denny had been off in town and had bumped into Wickham, apparently by chance. He then invited Wickham to join the regiment as an officer. Wickham agreed and came to Meryton, where he promptly met Lydia in the street. Although it is not stated, there must have been an opening for Wickham to fill. Presumably either the regiment had left its home county one officer short or - more likely - an officer had fallen sick

Wickham and Elizabeth dining together at Longbourn from a 19th century edition of the book. Wickham is shown in uniform, which is correct for an off-duty army officer at this date. Naval officers, however, were not allowed to wear their uniforms when not on active service.

Jane Austen and the Military

or left for some reason. This sort of sudden opening would account for Colonel Forster accepting Wickham as an officer based on nothing more than his appearance and Denny's friendship - and as we readers later discover that was a very new friendship indeed.

Denny himself is something less than entirely reputable. He is mentioned only 12 times in the book. Almost exclusively he is mentioned in connection with Wickham and has no clearly defined character. He is obviously young and possibly rather more reckless and less careful than his family would want.

In Chapter 47 we learn that Denny told Colonel Forster that he thought that when Wickham eloped with Lydia he had not intention at all of marrying the girl nor of taking her to Gretna Green. It would have been the bounden duty of any respectable young man who had such suspicions to warn the girl in question and, if she did not believe him, to go to her family. Yet, Denny did neither. He only told of his suspicions when questioned by Colonel Forster, his commanding officer. This is not proper behaviour and casts some doubt on Denny's character.

In Chapter 49, when Mr Gardiner is searching for Wickham and Lydia, he learns of Wickham that "It was not known that Wickham had a single relationship with whom he kept up any connection ... "His former acquaintances had been numerous; but since he had been in the militia, it did not appear that he was on terms of particular friendship with any of them."

In Austen's day this would have been very unusual behaviour in a young man, and one that would have immediately aroused suspicion - far more than it would today. Young men and women relied very much on family and friends to hear of good job or marriage prospects, and for personal recommendations. Anyone thinking of hiring a young person to do a job would have sought out recommendations and references. Back in the early 19th century this was taken very seriously.

Unlike today, when references are given lightly and taken just as

Jane Austen and the Military

non-seriously, recommendations were a matter of honour. If you gave a reference for somebody you were pledging your own honour and reputation on the accuracy of that reference. Should you declare somebody to be "honest" when they later turned out to be anything but it would be taken as a serious black mark against your own reputation and, indeed, your own honesty.

And recommendations were used much more widely. Anybody travelling to a strange part of the county would try to find somebody who knew a person there. Carrying a letter of recommendation, the traveller could arrive at their destination knowing that they had somewhere to stay, somebody who would cover incidental expenses and somebody who would, in turn, make useful introductions.

By avoiding contact with his old friends, Wickham was throwing away what should have been an extremely useful network of contacts, support and advantage. At this date nobody would do such a thing, unless they had something very serious to hide - as indeed Wickham did.

Instead, Wickham used his position as an officer of the militia to impress people and to act as an introduction and a recommendation. The hapless tradesmen of Meryton assumed that Wickham had been known to his fellow officers - gentlemen every one of them - for years and so could be relied upon to pay his debts in due course.

From what we learn of Wickham and his militia regiment in Pride and Prejudice it would seem that Jane Austen has faithfully and accurately given a picture of a militia regiment at this date. There is much she has missed out, but that is understandable. Austen was not interested in the minutiae of drilling, firing muskets or preparing to receive cavalry. She was interested in the officers, their social status and the impact that the arrival of these exotic and exciting creatures would have had on a small country town like Meryton.

And she got that spot on.

Jane Austen and the Military

Chapter 3
Colonel Fitzwilliam and the Purchase System

(Pride & Prejudice)

Colonel Fitzwilliam is a fairly minor character in Pride and Prejudice. He does not appear until Chapter 31 and is gone by Chapter 37. Although his presence is rather fleeting, he is important for the development of the storyline. His main role is to inadvertently refer to the way Darcy has earlier broken up the budding romance between Bingley and Jane, not realising that he is talking to Jane's sister Elizabeth. This serves to increase Elizabeth's dislike of Darcy.

Having successfully delivered himself of his required role in the plot, Colonel Fitzwilliam departs never to be seen again. Nevertheless he does bring up a most peculiar aspect of the military in Austen's time: the Purchase System.

We first meet Colonel Fitzwilliam when Elizabeth is visiting her friend, Charlotte, recently married to the vicar William Collins. Soon after she arrives, the Collins household is visited by Darcy, who brings *with him another man. This turns out to be "a Colonel Fitzwilliam, the younger son of his uncle Lord ——,"* When the pair enter the room, Austen continues "Colonel Fitzwilliam, who led the way, was about thirty, not handsome, but in person and address most truly the gentleman." And a bit later *"Colonel Fitzwilliam entered into conversation directly with the readiness and ease of a well-bred man, and talked very pleasantly".*

Jane Austen and the Military

In due course we learn that Colonel Fitzwilliam is a cousin of Darcy, making him a nephew of both of Lady Catherine de Bourgh and Lady Anne Darcy. He is also, along with Darcy, the co-guardian of Miss Georgiana Darcy - an earlier target of the unscrupulous attentions of the cad Wickham. If these facts and family connections do not mark him out for the reader as being a very grand personage,

An illustration showing a British infantry regiment being attacked by a French column. The British habitually formed in a line formation with the men formed up only two or three ranks deep. This allowed all the men to fire simultaneously, but made moving around the battlefield slow and difficult. The French preferred to form up in columns which could more much more quickly, but had restricted firepower. Note the British officer in the foreground. He is standing on the extreme right of the line to control movements and firing on this flank, and is therefore the major. Behind him stands a corproal armed with a pike. The colonel would have been standing, or possibly sitting on his horse, immediately behind the centre of the regimental line.

Jane Austen and the Military

we learn that his father is an earl - though his title is not given in the book.

It might be thought that as a colonel and the son of an earl, Fitzwilliam would be an ideal marriage prospect for the Bennett girls, but alas not. Fitzwilliam himself explains his predicament in a conversation with Elizabeth in Chapter 34. Elizabeth speaks first in this exchange:

> *"Do you certainly leave Kent on Saturday?" said she.*
>
> *"Yes—if Darcy does not put it off again. But I am at his disposal. He arranges the business just as he pleases."*
>
> *"And if not able to please himself in the arrangement, he has at least pleasure in the great power of choice. I do not know anybody who seems more to enjoy the power of doing what he likes than Mr. Darcy."*
>
> *"He likes to have his own way very well," replied Colonel Fitzwilliam. "But so we all do. It is only that he has better means of having it than many others, because he is rich, and many others are poor. I speak feelingly. A younger son, you know, must be inured to self-denial and dependence."*
>
> *"In my opinion, the younger son of an earl can know very little of either. Now seriously, what have you ever known of self-denial and dependence? When have you been prevented by want of money from going wherever you chose, or procuring anything you had a fancy for?"*
>
> *"These are home questions—and perhaps I cannot say that I have experienced many hardships of that nature. But in matters "of greater weight, I may suffer from want of money. Younger sons cannot marry where they like."*
>
> *"Unless where they like women of fortune, which I think they very often do."*
>
> *"Our habits of expense make us too dependent, "and there are not many in my rank of life who can afford to marry without some attention to money."*

Jane Austen and the Military

So, the situation in which the 30-year-old Colonel Fitzwilliam finds himself is that he is the younger son of an earl without money and in need of a rich wife. Whether this is a tactful way of letting Elizabeth down gently or not we are left to wonder.

What is of interest to the military aspect of the man is that he had attained the rank of colonel while in his twenties, but was no longer on the active list. Austen does not specifically say that Fitzwilliam is an inactive soldier, but with the war against France raging at full tilt he would almost certainly have been needed in the field if he were active.

At the time the book is set, Wellington was triumphant in Spain. He crushed the main French field army in Spain at Vitoria in June 1813 and captured the key fortress-port of San Sebastian in August. Those victories allowed him to drive the French out of most of Spain by the end of September. Together with his Portuguese and Spanish allies, Wellington was poised to invade France by marching over the Pyrenees. The army was mustering full strength for the invasion of France and every officer was needed in Spain. And yet Fitzwilliam is in England.

The other slight mystery that Austen does not address directly, largely because her audience would have been able to guess, is how a young man reached the exalted rank of colonel while still so young.

The answer, to a reader in 1813, would have been obvious. His family had bought the rank for him with cold hard cash.

The younger son of an earl could expect to inherit absolutely nothing, no matter how wealthy his family might be. In the early 19th century the custom of primogeniture ruled supreme. This meant that when a man died his entire wealth and estate was passed on to his eldest legitimate son. If there were no legitimate son, it would go to the eldest daughter. If there were no daughter it would pass to his younger brother, or if no brother to a sister and if no sister to the nearest male cousin or lacking that to a female cousin. The key point was that all the wealth was passed on as one single entity. No wealth

Jane Austen and the Military

was split away from the central family estate to provide for younger siblings.

In England this was not always the case. Many men made what were known as "settlements" on younger sons or on daughters. Generally a settlement would be a cash sum. For a member of the landed aristocracy it would have been unthinkable to split up the actual estates that went with the title.

The system had its advantages and disadvantages. For those immediately involved, the situation was clear. The heir got the lot. The rest got nothing. For society as a whole the picture was more mixed. Primogeniture meant that the main economic units in a basically agricultural economy remained intact. There are important advantages of scale in any business, allowing larger concerns to operate more efficiently than smaller units. When large estates of land - and we must assume that the Fitzwilliam estates were huge if the owner was an earl - remained intact they would have been generally well run. This boosted employment for the poor, tax revenues for the government and cash flow for the nobility. It also ensured stability and permanence. Most noble families at this date considered it their duty to use their accrued wealth to care for their tenants and local tradesmen in hard times. That reduced the likelihood of riots or unrest - even revolution.

On the other hand the concentration of huge wealth in the hands of a few meant that the local poor were dependent on the goodwill of their local noble. If that noble were sensible, benevolent and sane then all was well, but a vicious, greedy or mad nobleman could play real havoc with lives of the locals and there was precious little that they could do about it.

When it came to younger sons, such as Colonel Fitzwilliam, the family were highly unlikely to leave him completely in the lurch. It is made clear that he could look forward to no cash settlement from his father. That was not at all uncommon, but the father would make provision in some other way. Using his connections, social prestige

Jane Austen and the Military

and ready cash a nobleman could secure a comfortable future for his younger children. Girls could be married to rich men, while sons could be helped into a respectable career in the Church, government or armed forces.

It was clearly this latter route that he anonymous earl had chosen for his younger son, Colonel Fitzwilliam. No doubt the young man would have been consulted about his desired career path, but once the army had been settled upon then the family money could be used to buy him his position as a colonel. This was a system known as "purchase", and was entirely proper and respectable in the early 19th Century. It might seem odd and frankly disgraceful to us today that a man could buy his way into any sort of a job for cash - still less into a highly responsible job such as being an army officer - but at the time it seemed perfectly normal and, indeed, preferable to the alternatives.

The purchase system had its origins way back in the later middle ages. England had no army back then. When a king went to war - either to fight off invasion or to invade another country [usually France] - he turned to his noblemen for support. They in turn looked to the farmers and tenants on their estates. Adventurous young men were recruited into a military unit, the size of which varied considerably depending on the wealth of the nobleman or knight concerned. Some knights went to war with just themselves and a squire or two. Richer noblemen could field what were effectively small private armies numbering in their thousands.

The costs of all this fell on the noblemen doing the recruiting. It was they who paid for uniforms, weapons, supplies and transport carts. They also paid the wages of the soldiers who had been recruited - the going rate for an archer in the 14th century was three pence per day, while a knight could expect to be paid two shillings per day. Getting a military unit into the field, and keeping it supplied and healthy, was a very expensive business.

In theory at least the noblemen was reimbursed by the king, but it was rare indeed for any monarch to pay the full amount. At any rate,

Jane Austen and the Military

the king paid a flat rate that was only just enough to equip men with the most basic of weapons and equipment. If he were to attract good soldiers, and keep them, a leader had to provide good quality equipment - and that cost money. All the weapons and other equipment belonged to the nobleman who had paid the bills in the first place. When the campaign was over, he was free to sell the surplus equipment or to keep it for the next time. Castles and manors the length and breadth of the country had swords, spears, helmets and suits of armour hanging on their walls. They were therefore both ready for instant use and to act as very obvious proof that the owner had served the king in war and was a man of prestige, wealth and honour.

It was also possible for a commander to sell his unit to another commander. In this instance there was no compulsion for the men to switch allegiance to the new commander, though most usually did.

This informal system fell apart in the 17th century in truly spectacular fashion. When Parliament and King went to war in 1642, both sides rushed to raise armies in the traditional manner. Fairly quickly, however, Parliament changed things. They created what they dubbed "The New Model Army". A highly professional force that was regularly paid, highly disciplined and magnificently equipped. It turned out to be both their wisest and most foolish move.

The New Model Army swept across Britain, crushing the Royalist

A German illustration showing British infantry officers of various ranks and from different regiments as they were during the Waterloo Campaign of 1815. The man sitting down is a colonel, as shown by his two epaulettes and the gorget - the crescent-shaped metal plate hanging below his throat.

45

Jane Austen and the Military

forces with ease. Parliament was jubilant; they had won the English Civil War. But then the army turned on Parliament. The soldiers and their officers reckoned that since they had done all the fighting, they should get to make the decisions about how Britain should be run now peace had come.

In December 1648 the New Model Army marched on Parliament. In all 45 MPs were arrested and thrown in prison, while another 250 were thrown out of Parliament at sword point and banned from attending in future. Shortly afterwards King Charles was executed and the army's chosen favourite general, Oliver Cromwell, was installed with what amounted to dictatorial powers.

It was a military coup that starkly showed that a civilian government was helpless in the face of determined armed force.

When Charles's son was restored to the throne in 1660, one of his first moves to was take steps to ensure that a military coup could never again succeed. The system of purchase was part of this wider plan.

The system drew on the old methods of raising armies. It was decided that, in theory, the regiment's uniforms, equipment and supplies all belonged to the colonel. It was he who had to pay all the bills, though he was later reimbursed by the government for his expenses. The first colonel of a regiment did, indeed, pay for the raising of the regiment along with all its equipment.

Men who wanted to serve as officers in a new regiment had to pay a cash sum to the Crown for the privilege. When they retired or got promoted, they could sell their commission as an officer to somebody else. So a man serving as a lieutenant who wanted to be promoted to be a captain would simultaneously pay to purchase the commission as a captain, and sell his commission as a lieutenant - which served in part to offset the cost of his new commission.

The cost of a commission was significant, a deliberate step to ensure that only rich men could serve as offices. By the time of Pride and Prejudice it cost about £450 to become an ensign in an infantry regiment, £700 to be a lieutenant, £1,800 to be a captain, £3,200 to

Jane Austen and the Military

be a major and no less than £4,500 to reach Fitzwilliam's rank of Colonel. In a cavalry regiment the equivalent ranks sold for: £840; £1,190; £3,225; £4,575 and £6,175. In the guards regiments the prices were even higher.

In addition to these official figures, there would often be unofficial bonus payments. A commission in a fashionable regiment cost two or three times that of an unfashionable regiment. And regiments ordered to go to far distant parts of the world, such as the West Indies, were cheaper than those serving at home.

Given that the average workman would be paid around £20 per year, these were massive sums of money.

It is worth noting that only regimental ranks could be purchased - meaning that colonel was the highest rank that could be bought. What were known as general officers, those more senior to the rank of colonel, could not be purchased. Promotion to the ranks such as brigadier, major general, lieutenant general, general and field marshal were made solely on the basis of merit, though often luck and good contacts among the noble families with a military background also helped.

The high cost of a purchased commission was treated by the Crown as a form of bond for good behaviour. Any officer found guilty of serious military crimes - desertion, mutiny or incompetence - would be "cashiered". This meant that they were stripped of their rank without being allowed to sell their commission. In other words, they lost the money they had paid for the commission.

This was not the only advantage for the crown in the purchase system. The high cost of entry meant that only wealthy men could become officers. By definition those would be men who had a vested interest in preserving the status quo. Wealthy men are generally those who have done well out of the present system and so have no material interest in seeing it overthrown. Unlike the religious zealots from the middle classes who made up the officer corps of the New Model Army in 1648, the new style officers would be drawn from the upper

Jane Austen and the Military

classes. They could therefore be trusted with commanding armed men, as they were unlikely to back a rebellion or revolution.

There were other advantages too. A man who was wealthy in his own right was unlikely to take advantage of the opportunities for bribery and corruption that presented themselves. Officers were responsible for equipping and supplying their men, being later reimbursed by the government. There would have been temptations to equip the men with cheap, substandard muskets and poor quality food, then charge the government for top quality goods using fraudulent paperwork. No doubt some greedy officers did just that, but it was thought that wealthy men were less likely to fall victim to temptation.

This was absolutely crucial in the army. When men go into battle they are risking their lives. If they know that their muskets are unlikely to fire properly they are not likely to do much in the way of actual fighting. Instead they will flee or surrender as soon as the enemy comes in sight. No soldier was willing to get himself killed just so his commanding officer could make some extra money fiddling the accounts.

Another secondary advantage was that wealthy officers were less likely to take part in, or allow their men to take part in, looting and pillage. Again, this was crucial in battle. If soldiers stop to steal from the bodies of the dead they will miss out on opportunities to inflict serious defeats on the enemy.

Moreover nothing is more likely to stir up a civilian population against an army than if the soldiers steal, pillage and rape as they march along. A wealthy officer with no need to steal himself was less likely to allow his men to do so. That would keep the local civilian population friendly.

Organised extortion was another matter entirely. When marching through enemy territory it was not at all unusual for commanders to extort food, other supplies and even money as "voluntary contributions" from the local civilians. There was nothing voluntary

Jane Austen and the Military

about it, of course, for the threat of violence was always present. Such benefits were passed on down the ranks. Similarly valuables taken from the enemy dead would be shared out.

Given the type of society that existed in England in the 1660s there were other advantages to having an officer class made up entirely of wealthy gentlemen from good families. Although English society as this date was considerably more mobile than that in other European countries, it was still that case that farm labourers and others from the lower classes looked up to the upper classes in most civilian circumstances. In the army a private drawn from the labouring class was likely to obey an order from the son of an earl quicker and more readily than an order from another plough boy. On the field of battle when quick reactions could spell the difference between victory or defeat, life or death, that was important.

By the time that Jane Austen was writing, English society was changing. Merchants, industrialists and factory owners were filling out the ranks of both the wealthy and the super rich. No longer were the richest people in the country the big landowners and high ranking noblemen. Many a factory owner was richer than any knight or lord. The social exclusivity of the army officers made this a useful route to social acceptance open to the sons of mine owners or mill owners who would otherwise be excluded from the social salons of the nobility.

During the Peninsular War many Spanish officers - themselves almost exclusively drawn from the old noble families - were surprised and aghast to learn that the British officers they dined with were the sons of men who owned cotton weaving businesses or coal mines.

Despite these many advantages to the government, the purchase system was never one of pure cash for rank. Any man wishing to purchase a commission had to be approved by both the colonel of the regiment and by the monarch (the monarch usually delegated this task to a committee of senior officers at Horse Guards). This should ensure that completely unsuitable candidates did not get into positions of

Jane Austen and the Military

command, though it did not always work out that way.

Nor was it possible for somebody to walk in from civilian life and purchase the colonelcy of a regiment. Every officer had to start as an ensign and work his way up through the ranks. There were minimum lengths of time that had to be served in each rank before it was permitted to purchase the next rank up. These varied over they years, but were rarely less than two years. It would therefore take a minimum of ten years to go from ensign to colonel. Given that nobody was allowed to be an ensign until they were 16 years old, that meant that the youngest possible age to be a colonel was 26. This was exceptional and it was more normal for a colonel to be in his thirties or forties.

In any case there were always commissions that could be gained by merit, or good luck, rather than by paying cold hard cash. Within each regiment there were a number of non-purchase commissions that could be filled by the colonel, though every such appointment had to be approved by the monarch. In addition to these non-purchase commissions, it was also the custom that any commission that fell vacant due to the holder being killed in action or promoted to the general staff were also filled at the discretion of the colonel and without a purchase price being paid - though in these cases the newly promoted officer could sell his commission at the regular price when he chose to move on in due course.

Operating on the fringes of this system were the men termed "gentleman rankers". These were young men from good families who were unable to afford the price of purchasing a commission, but who were otherwise suited to be officers. They joined the army as privates - meaning that they served in the ranks along with the men. But as gentlemen they were obviously from a higher social class than most rankers, and usually had considerably more money than the other privates. They might even pay to mess with the officers - so joining the officers for meals and sharing their sleeping arrangements.

These gentlemen-rankers were usually serving in the hope of

Jane Austen and the Military

getting a non-purchase commission. If they could catch the eye of the colonel by devotion to duty, hard work, efficiency and reckless bravery they were likely to find themselves promoted up to the next non-purchase ensignship that fell vacant. It was a viable way into the officer class for younger sons unable to rely on their family for the money needed to purchase.

Finally there were officers who were promoted from the ranks. This was a rather unusual move, but became less so as the continuing war led to an increased demand for officers. To qualify, a man had to have reached the rank of sergeant, have an unblemished record and be able to read and write. That ruled out most men, but even so a fair number of able sergeants were promoted into non-purchase commissions by their colonels. Reliable figures are hard to come by, but by the time Pride and Prejudice was published as many as 10% of officers in the British army may have been promoted from the ranks.

Some readers might be familiar with one such officer in the shape of the fictional Richard Sharpe - hero of a series of novels by Bernard Cornwall. In these novels a mainspring of the plot is often the snobbery that Sharpe encounters from posh officers who have bought their commissions and who look down on the guttersnipe Sharpe.

Such social conflicts could and did occur, but officers raised from the ranks were more often likely to run into financial problems. In a smart regiment in which all the officers came from monied families, the mess bill of an officer could easily be higher than his actual salary. That would be a quick route to bankruptcy for an officer with no income other than his pay. For this reason most officers raised from the ranks tended to serve in less fashionable regiments, and in any case rarely rose above the rank of captain - though the fictional Sharpe got to Lieutenant Colonel.

So turning back to Pride and Prejudice's Colonel Fitzwilliam, we can see that Austen has provided us with a sketchy but entirely believable snapshot of military life.

Jane Austen and the Military

As the son of an earl, Fitzwilliam could have relied upon his family to set him up in a career. It would therefore have been natural for them to have purchased him a commission in the army. Given his age of about 30 it was entirely possible for him to have reached the rank of Colonel. On the other hand, he would have had no money of his own other than his salary, while his position in society would have demanded more of him. For this reason he would have been on the look out for a wealthy heiress, not one of the Bennett girls.

Once again, Austen hits the bull's eye on military matters.

Jane Austen and the Military

Chapter 4
William Price and family influence

(Mansfield Park)

With William Price we leave the army and move to the Royal Navy. In Jane Austen's time the Royal Navy was far more important than was the army. While the militia provided a security blanket in the form of home defence and the army marched across the Iberian Peninsula, the navy carried Britain's power and might right around the world. And while the army won important victories, the great battles fought by the Royal Navy changed world history and dominated the newspapers.

And the Royal Navy was huge. In 1814, the year that Mansfield Park was published, the Royal Navy was by a wide margin the most powerful navy in the world. It dominated the seas of the world in a way that no navy has done before or since.

In that year the Royal Navy could put to sea no less than 118 big warships able to take their place in the "line of battle" during a major engagement against other warships. Most of these were two deckers mounting the conventional 74 cannon. But 15 ships were three deckers mounting up to 120 cannon. Another 144 ships were rated as warships that were expected to take the fight to the enemy. These smaller ships had only one deck of guns, and mounted between 24 and 56 guns. They were fast, sleek craft that raced around capturing enemy merchant ships, despatching pirates and cruising the oceans to seek and destroy His Majesty's enemies. Smaller still were the

Jane Austen and the Military

sloops, brigs and cutters that mounted between 6 and 22 guns. These craft were used for a vast multitude of tasks right around the world. Then there were specialist craft such as the 10 bomb vessels which could cruise up rivers to lob massive exploding shells into enemy cities. Another 28 ships were fitted out to carry army units - including horses, wagons and guns - to foreign parts. There were even 3 ships designed to do nothing but surveys of the waters and coasts of the world.

In all the Royal Navy in 1814 had 697 ships and over 100,000 men at sea. Today the Royal Navy has just 77 ships, of which only 19 can be considered to be major warships. Even the navy of the USA, today's mightiest fleet, can boast only 430 ships.

Not only did the Royal Navy dominate in terms of numbers, it went where no other navy dared to venture. It had been a Royal Navy ship that was the first to penetrate the Antarctic Circle, it was the Royal Navy that explored the Australian coast and landed colonists there, and it was Royal Navy ships that ventured into Polynesia. And where the Royal Navy went, the Royal Navy imposed British control of the trade routes.

But the Royal Navy was a very different creature to the Army. Back in the 17th Century it had been the army, not the navy, which had taken part in the coup that overthrew the government. Moreover, the high cost of building and fitting out a warship meant that all but the smallest were beyond the pocket of a private citizen. Big warships cost big money, and only the government could afford them. Naval officers had always been directly dependent on the monarch and government for their livelihoods and chances of promotion. There was no doubt about their loyalty, so there was no real requirement for the sort of bond for good behaviour that was the official reason for the purchase of commissions in the army.

Not only that, but the skills of a naval officer were very different from those of an army officer. An army officer needed to be brave, loyal and have that indefinable quality of leadership that mean his

Jane Austen and the Military

men would follow him into battle. But a naval officer needed more than mere courage and leadership skills. He also needed to know how to navigate a ship, sail a ship and deal with the thousand and one technical problems that could be thrown up taking a wooden craft thousands of miles over the oceans through storms, calms and shoals.

And so we come to William Price in the novel Mansfield Park. As the novel opens he is aged 10 and is the eldest child of the impoverished Price family. He is, therefore, the elder brother of the novel's heroine Fanny Price, aged 9 when the story begins. The family owes its poverty - or at least "poverty" in comparison to the majority

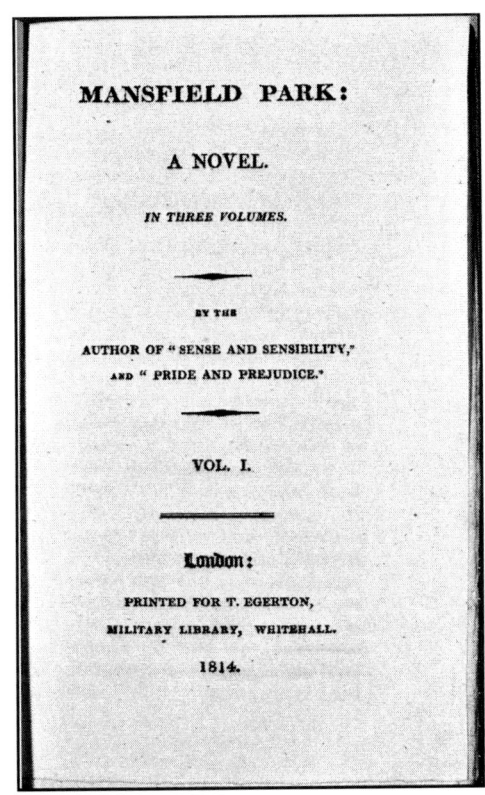

The title page of the first edition of Mansfield Park. Despite being Austen's third novel, it was widely ignored when it first came out with none of the usual literary magazines bothering to review it at all.

Jane Austen and the Military

of gentle folk who made up Austen's world - to a combination of low income and high expenditure.

As time passes Sir Thomas Bertram continues to take an interest in the Price children. Austen covers William's entrance into the Royal Navy in a rather vague manner. In Chapter 2 she writes the following:

"Amid the cares and the complacency which his own children suggested, Sir Thomas did not forget to do what he could for the children of Mrs. Price: he assisted her liberally in the education and disposal of her sons as they became old enough for a determinate pursuit; and Fanny, though almost totally separated from her family, was sensible of the truest satisfaction in hearing of any kindness towards them, or of anything at all promising in their situation or conduct. Once, and once only, in the course of many years, had she the happiness of being with William. Of the rest she saw nothing: nobody seemed to think of her ever going amongst them again, even for a visit, nobody at home seemed to want her; but William determining, soon after her removal, to be a sailor, was invited to spend a week with his sister in Northamptonshire before he went to sea. Their eager affection in meeting, their exquisite delight in being together, their hours of happy mirth, and moments of serious conference, may be imagined; as well as the sanguine views and spirits of the boy even to the last, and the misery of the girl when he left her. Luckily the visit happened in the Christmas holidays, when she could directly look for comfort to her cousin Edmund; and he told her such charming things of what William was to do, and be hereafter, in consequence of his profession, as made her gradually admit that the separation might have some use. Edmund's friendship never failed her: his leaving Eton for Oxford made no change in his kind dispositions, and only afforded more frequent opportunities of proving them. Without any display of doing more than the rest, or any fear of doing too much, he was

Jane Austen and the Military

always true to her interests, and considerate of her feelings, trying to make her good qualities understood, and to conquer the diffidence which prevented their being more apparent; giving her advice, consolation, and encouragement."

The Edmund referred to here is the younger son of the Bertrams.

All we learn of William at this point is that he is leaving to "be a sailor". In Chapter 5 we learn that William is abroad somewhere for Austen tells us of Fanny that "Upon the whole, it was a comfortable winter to her; for though it brought no William to England, the never-failing hope of his arrival was worth much."

After various passing references to William, it is not until Chapter 16 that we finally learn for certain that William is in the Royal Navy, not serving on a merchant ship. Austen is describing Fanny's small attic bedroom with its meagre furniture and tatty decorative state. Almost in passing she tells us that among the assorted pictures and decorative features were:

"a collection of family profiles, thought unworthy of being anywhere else, over the mantelpiece, and by their side, and pinned against the wall, a small "sketch of a ship sent four years ago from the Mediterranean by William, with H.M.S. Antwerp at the bottom, in letters as tall as the mainmast."

With its prefix of "H.M.S", meaning His Majesty's Ship, the Antwerp must be a ship in the Royal Navy. There was no such ship in the Royal Navy during the Napoleonic Wars. There was an HMS Antwerp in the Second World War, possibly named by a fan of Jane Austen's writing, but she was a different vessel.

What type of vessel HMS Antwerp is supposed to be, we are never told. It must have been a fairly substantial ship for at one point we are told that she had a Chaplain on board. On smaller ships one of the officers, often the Captain, presided over Sunday religious services, funerals and the like. We also learn that the Antwerp is spending most of its time in the Mediterranean, but what it is doing there we do not know.

Jane Austen and the Military

In Chapter 24 William comes to visit Fanny. HMS Antwerp is at this time anchored at Spithead, off Portsmouth, and William has some leave ashore. It is at this point that we learn that William "was still only a midshipman" despite having been at sea for seven years. Speaking of William's visit, Austen tells us that:

"Sir Thomas had the pleasure of receiving, in his protégé, certainly a very different person from the one he had equipped seven years ago, but a young man of an open, pleasant countenance, and frank, unstudied, but feeling and respectful manners, and such as confirmed him his friend."

A midshipman in the Royal Navy. Note that he carries the sextant that he was learning to use to navigate a ship and his personal log in which he recorded everything he did for the inspection of his senior officers. He wears a blue coat as befits his status as a would-be officer, but he lacks the wide lapels which denoted a naval officer.

Jane Austen and the Military

At last we are able to put the pieces together, though it must be said that Austen has not made it easy for a reader to understand William's career to date. Even a contemporary reader might have been somewhat puzzled.

Clearly what had happened was that Sir Thomas Bertram had used his contacts and friendships to get young William a position in the Royal Navy as a midshipman. This was a normal route into the navy for a young gentleman aiming for a career as an officer. The name of this rank refers to the fact that the young men were not yet officers, but being destined for that rank were not ordinary sailors either. Their actual position on the ladder or ranks was ambiguous. Officially they were less important than several of the sailors, but at other times could be put in command of men technically superior to themselves. Traditionally a warship had the quarters for the officers at the rear of the ship and those of the sailors at the front. So the trainee offices had their quarters in the middle of the ship - hence the term "midshipmen".

The details of William's progress are not given, but we know what was typical. First a boy aged between 8 and 14 who aspired to be a naval officer would join a ship in some unofficial capacity. This might be as an officer's servant, a secretary or personal cook. It was here that the role of family connections came into play. For a boy to go to sea, he had to be invited to do so by a serving officer. There were usually more boys wanting to join a ship than there were places available, so officers had could pick and choose who they took on. It was possible, though rare, for a boy to serve out this early stage in his career on shore. If a captain could be persuaded to enter the boy on to his ship's muster without him actually being there then he would, on paper at any rate, have served his first few years. By the time Austen was writing this practice was extremely rare and was considered improper, not just by the naval authorities but by most officers as well.

Any sort of patronage or influence would help. The great Admiral Nelson, for instance, got his start when taken aboard HMS

Jane Austen and the Military

Raisonnable by his maternal uncle, Maurice Suckling. It is clear by the way Austen terms William to be Sir Thomas Bertram's "protégé" that it had been Bertram who had persuaded some officer to take young William aboard as a Volunteer.

Austen also tells us that Sir Thomas had "equipped" William when he first went aboard. This will have meant that he provided William with a sea chest, clothing, books, notebooks, pens, ink and a host of other materials that he would need.

By the time William joined, this unofficial system had gained some sort of formal recognition for such boys were enrolled on to the ship's company as "Volunteers" and paid 10 shillings per lunar month. Although they might have some duties owed to their officer, their main task was to learn as much as they could about life aboard a warship.

After a period of time, the boys might be taken on to the ship's company with the rank of Midshipman. This was entirely in the gift of the captain. If he thought that the boy was totally unsuited to a life at sea, he was quite at liberty to send the boy back home. This was, however, rare and the majority of Volunteers could expect to become Midshipmen after a year or two.

By the time William became a midshipman around half of those holding this rank were the sons of middle class families. Around 20 per cent were the off spring of the landed gentry or nobility and the rest came from a variety of backgrounds - including sailors promoted to the rank for good service or because their captain recognised their talents. As a result the midshipmen in a ship could be a very mixed bunch regarding both age and social background. Indeed, the future King William IV served as a midshipman for five years.

As a midshipman, William reports to Fanny that he has a rough time. When Fanny asks him if he would rather be at Portsmouth, William tells her:

"No, Fanny, that I do not. I shall have enough of Portsmouth and of dancing too, when I cannot have you. And I do not know

Jane Austen and the Military

that there would be any good in going to the assembly, for I might not get a partner. The Portsmouth girls turn up their noses at anybody who has not a commission. One might as well be nothing as a midshipman. One is nothing, indeed. You remember the Gregorys; they are grown up amazing fine girls, but they will hardly speak to me, because Lucy is courted by a lieutenant."

On another occasion it is suggested that when William gets back to Portsmouth he might care to call on some grand relatives living in Brighton. He responds:

"I should be very happy, aunt; but Brighton is almost by Beachey Head; and if I could get so far, I could not expect to be welcome in such a smart place as that—poor scrubby midshipman as I am."

William is, we can assume, giving his view of the status of a midshipman here. And he is not too far of the mark. Midshipmen were considered to be apprentices or students and so had very little status themselves.

On board ship, midshipmen had to learn a vast number of skills that they would need if they were to be officers. They were taught to rig sails, other duties included keeping watch, relaying messages between decks, supervising gun batteries, commanding small boats, and taking command of a sub-division of the ship's company under the supervision of one of the lieutenants. They would also be taught the complicated mathematics and arcane skills needed to navigate a ship by taking sightings on the stars or the sun. They had to keep detailed logs - or diaries - in which they wrote everything they did. These were marked by the supervising lieutenant and served as the official record of the boy's education at sea.

The next news we have of the career of the absent William Price comes in Chapter 31. Henry Crawford visits Mansfield Park to see Fanny. After a brief chat with Lady Bertram, who then leaves, Henry turns to Fanny. Austen continues:

Jane Austen and the Military

"Henry, overjoyed to have her go, bowed and watched her off, and without losing another moment, turned instantly to Fanny, and, taking out some letters, said, with a most animated look, "I must acknowledge myself infinitely obliged to any creature who gives me such an opportunity of seeing you alone: I have been wishing it more than you can have any idea. Knowing as I do what your feelings as a sister are, I could hardly have borne that any one in the house should share with you in the first knowledge of the news I now bring. He is made. Your brother is a lieutenant. I have the infinite satisfaction of congratulating you on your brother's promotion. Here are the letters which announce it, this moment come to hand. You will, perhaps, like to see them."

Fanny could not speak, but he did not want her to speak. To see the expression of her eyes, the change of her complexion, the progress of her feelings, their doubt, confusion, and felicity, was enough. She took the letters as he gave them. The first was from the Admiral to inform his nephew, in a few words, of his having succeeded in the object he had undertaken, the promotion of young Price, and enclosing two more, one from the Secretary of the First Lord to a friend, whom the Admiral had set to work in the business, the other from that friend to himself, by which it appeared that his lordship had the very great happiness of attending to the recommendation of Sir Charles; that Sir Charles was much delighted in having such an opportunity of proving his regard for Admiral Crawford, and that the circumstance of Mr. William Price's commission as Second Lieutenant of H.M. Sloop Thrush being made out was spreading general joy through a wide circle of great people."

After some further discussion, Crawford then seeks to claim the credit for William's promotion for himself:

"Henry was most happy to make it more intelligible, by

Jane Austen and the Military

beginning at an earlier stage, and explaining very particularly what he had done. His last journey to London had been undertaken with no other view than that of introducing her brother in Hill Street, and prevailing on the Admiral to exert whatever interest he might have for getting him on. This had been his business. He had communicated it to no creature: he had not breathed a syllable of it even to Mary; while uncertain of the issue, he could not have borne any participation of his feelings, but this had been his business; and he spoke with such a glow of what his solicitude had been, and used such strong expressions, was so abounding in the deepest interest, in twofold motives, in views and wishes more than could be told, that Fanny could not have remained insensible of his drift, had she been able to attend; but her heart was so full and her senses still so astonished, that she could listen but imperfectly even to what he told her of William, and saying only when he paused, "How kind! how very kind! Oh, Mr. Crawford, we are "infinitely obliged to you! Dearest, dearest William!" She jumped up and moved in haste towards the door, crying out, "I will go to my uncle. My uncle ought to know it as soon as possible." But this could not be suffered. The opportunity was too fair, and his feelings too impatient. He was after her immediately. "She must not go, she must allow him five minutes longer," and he took her hand and led her back to her seat, and was in the middle of his farther explanation, before she had suspected for what she was detained."

Crawford goes on to declare his love, only to be spurned by Fanny.

This account of how William got his promotion to the rank of lieutenant seems, on the face of it, to be relatively straightforward.

The "Admiral" referred to here is Admiral Crawford, the father of young Henry Crawford. The "Secretary to the First Lord", was the most senior official in the Admiralty. At this date, the Royal Navy was run by the Board of the Admiralty, which was composed of a

Jane Austen and the Military

number of worthies. The office was chaired, and in effect mostly under the control of, the First Lord of the Admiralty. This position was a political office and had the rank of a cabinet minister in the government. The First Lord was always a member of Parliament and usually, though not always, a man who had had at least some naval experience at sea earlier in his career.

At the date that Mansfield Park was published, the First Lord was Robert Dundas, Viscount Melville. He had never served at sea, but

A portrait of Robert Dundas, Viscount Melville, who was First Lord of the Admiralty at the time Mansfield Park was published. Whether or not he thought that the book was referring to him when it spoke of the First Lord is unrecorded. In all likelihood he never read the book.

Jane Austen and the Military

had represented the coastal towns of Hastings and Rye when he had been an MP and before he succeeded to his father's title and so entered the House of Lords. Although he had qualified as a lawyer as a young man, he spent nearly all of his career in government or diplomatic posts. It is, however, unlikely that Austen meant to refer to Melville when she spoke of the "First Lord". In the ten years before Mansfield Park was published there had been six First Lords, and it seemed likely that Melville's occupation of the office would be just as transitory - though in fact he remained in office until 1830.

Whichever First Lord was being referred to, the letter is said to have been written by his Secretary. This was, in effect, the head of the civil service within the Admiralty. When Mansfield Park was published the position was held by John Croker. This Irish man had a reputation for honesty, straight talking and integrity that he fully deserved. He was also something of a poet and a literary critic. As with Melville, he had only recently taken up his post and so it is unlikely that Austen intended for readers to think she referred to him personally.

Whether Austen had any particular First Lord or Secretary in mind, she clearly indicates that William's promotion to lieutenant was entirely due to their interest and interference in his career. While patronage from the top could certainly help a young man in the Royal Navy, it would have had very little to do with getting William promoted to be a lieutenant.

After some years as a midshipman, and having reached the age of 18, and assuming that he had completed three years as a midshipman and six years at sea, a young man was qualified to take the examination to become a real officer. These examinations took the form of an intense interview in front of a board of senior officers - usually three captains.

During this grilling, the midshipman was asked a vast number of questions on all sorts of maritime subjects. He had to be able to answer them promptly and correctly. After all, when a storm or enemy

Jane Austen and the Military

ship is bearing down a ship's officer has no margin for either error or delay.

At the end of the interview, the captains would retire in private to consider their verdict. If the midshipman failed the exam he would have to serve at least another six months at sea before he was allowed to take the exam again. Some midshipmen never passed the exam, despite trying repeated times. When they reached the age of 25 or 26 it was usually considered time that they moved on. Some might give up the navy and go ashore to try their luck elsewhere, but those who preferred to stay at sea had the chance to take on a variety of senior roles among the sailors.

Those who did pass the lieutenant's exam did not automatically become lieutenants. All the passing of the exam meant was that they were qualified to be a lieutenant when such a position became available. The midshipman might stay on as a "passed midshipman", but he was now qualified to take on a variety of roles on board ship. The best of these - and one that brought an increase in pay of around £1 per month - was that of Master's Mate.

A small ship would typically have two master's mates, one for each watch, while larger ships might have as many as six. Basically a master's mate acted as a deputy to the Ship's Master, the most senior non commissioned rank on board. He would be responsible for fitting out the ship, and making sure they had all the sailing supplies necessary for the voyage. They hoisted and lowered the anchor, and docked and undocked the ship. They would examine the ship daily, notifying the master if there were problems with the sails, masts, ropes, or pulleys. They executed the orders of the master, and would command in his place if he was sick or absent.

It was possible for the captain of a ship to promote a midshipman to be an acting lieutenant if a vacancy arose, but that would need to be confirmed by the admiral at some point. At the time of Mansfield Park, it was usual for a midshipman to have to wait about two years to become an lieutenant after having passed his exams.

Jane Austen and the Military

It is at this point that the support of the First Lord, Admiral Crawford and others would have been useful. They could have pressured a captain into giving a vacant position of lieutenant to young William - or have simply ordered his appointment to HMS Thrush.

It is noticeable, however, that Austen makes absolutely no mention at all of the exam that all midshipmen had to pass in order to qualify to be a lieutenant. Presumably she wanted to give all the credit to Henry Crawford, so that the debt of gratitude owed to him by Fanny would be all the greater. Fantastic as a plot device, but not all that accurate in terms of the reality of the Royal Navy at this date.

On the down side, however, being a lieutenant in a sloop was about as low a rung as a young man could hold and still be a lieutenant. And he was not even First Lieutenant, but the more junior Second Lieutenant. An officer's pay and his status depended on both his rank and what sort of a ship he served on. An officer on a really big line of battle ship could be paid more than twice as much as an officer of the same rank in a small ship - and William's ship was about as small as you could get.

At the time that Austen was writing Mansfield Park there really was an HMS Thrush in the Royal Navy. She was not, however, a dashing sloop in need of a lieutenant, but a hulk well passed her best being used to store gunpowder which anchored off Port Royal in Jamaica. A hulk was a ship which was still afloat but which was incapable of facing the open sea due to age or damage, or both. Typically a hulk would be anchored somewhere out the way, stripped of masts, sails and anything else of use and then used for some purpose until it fell apart, when it was scrapped. This particular HMS Thrush was used to store gunpowder and was anchored far enough off shore so that if there was an accident that resulted in the stored powder exploding no damage would be done to the town.

The ship that Austen had in mind, however, was an altogether much more exciting vessel for a young officer such as William Price.

Jane Austen and the Military

An armed sloop in naval service at this date would have been a fast ship of about 300 tons, armed with about 14 guns. When Mansfield Park was published the Royal Navy had no less than 222 armed sloops at sea. They were used to patrol coasts, carry messages, ferry senior officers around and a host of other duties that demanded speed and nimbleness.

William visits Fanny, and Fanny visits him in Portsmouth. Most of what happens between them refers to the plot of the novel, not to his career. The last we see of William he is still a lieutenant, although to be fair Austen does refer to "William's continued good conduct and rising fame".

Jane Austen and the Military

Looking at how Jane Austen portrayed in William Price the career of a young man hoping to be an officer in the Royal Navy we can see that she has not done too badly. Certainly she did not write anything that was actually incorrect. On the other hand her omission of the exam that had to be passed by all midshipmen is a serious one.

Facing page: A naval battle during the Napoleonic Wars. The ship in the centre is the huge French warship Ocean. She carried three decks of guns and had a total of 118 cannon on board, making her one of the largest and most powerful ships afloat at this time.

Jane Austen and the Military

Chapter 5
Mr Price and the Royal Marines

(Mansfield Park)

Having spent some time on young William Price and his fledgling career in the Royal Navy, it is now time to take a look at his father's rather longer but not especially successful career in the same service. We learn his back story very early in the novel, for as the father of the heroine, Fanny Price, his unfortunate career sets the scene for her own place in the world.

Having first established the existence of three sisters - Maria, Ward and Frances - of moderate fortune, Austen tells us of their matrimonial fortunes. That Maria married very well to Sir Thomas Bertram of Mansfield Park. Ward married a clergyman of modest means, but Frances "fared yet worse". Austen goes on to explain:

"Miss Frances married, in the common phrase, to disoblige her family, and by fixing on a lieutenant of marines, without education, fortune, or connexions, did it very thoroughly. She could hardly have made a more untoward choice. Sir Thomas Bertram had interest, which, from principle as well as pride—from a general wish of doing right, and a desire of seeing all that were connected with him in

Facing page: A private of the Royal Marines. Note that this man wears the army-style uniform that marked the marines out as being separate from the sailors. The narrow-brimmed tall hat was distinctive to the Royal Marines and was not shared by any army regiment.

Jane Austen and the Military

situations of respectability, he would have been glad to exert for the advantage of Lady Bertram's sister; but her husband's profession was such as no interest could reach."

The two elder sisters fall out with the foolish youngest one, after which pride and resentment stop them from communicating with each other. Austen continues:

> "By the end of eleven years, however, Mrs. Price could no longer afford to cherish pride or resentment, or to lose one connexion that might possibly assist her. A large and still

Jane Austen and the Military

increasing family, an husband disabled for active service, but not the less equal to company and good liquor".

And that is about all we are told about his naval career. We are not told how or when Mr Price was wounded, nor how serious his injuries were. Clearly they were bad enough for him to be retired from the marines on health grounds, but there is noticeable way in which his actions in the novel are hindered. He does not lack a limb, nor have trouble walking about town. Whatever his injuries were, they seem to have been of a remarkably non-visible kind.

We subsequently learn a lot about how Mr and Mrs Price lead their lives in the present day. They live in a small house, their home is pokey and dirty, their clothes are not fashionable, their manners are not of the best and so forth. Most of this seems to be inserted by Jane Austen to contrast Fanny's humble home with the grand, elegant and fashionable Mansfield Park.

Mr Price had been an officer of the Royal Marines, but he had become disabled in battle and so had been forced to retire from active service. We are told quite clearly that 11 years had passed from the marriage to the date when Fanny went to live at Mansfield Park, when she was 9 years old. Since Fanny is aged 19 at the close of the novel that would mean that the marriage had taken place 21 years before the end of the novel. Given that the book was published in 1814 then the very latest date for the marriage between Frances Ward and Lieutenant Price would have been 1793. Given the time it takes to write a novel, the date may have been intended to be a year or two earlier.

In 1790, the Royal Navy had consisted of 478 craft in total, of which 146 were big enough to take their place in the line during a major battle - though only 90 of those were fit to go to sea. That makes the peacetime Royal Navy of 1790 a little more than half as big as the war strength in 1814 when the novel was published.

The "Marine Forces" of 1790 - they did not become the Royal Marines until 1802 - were likewise fewer in number than they were

Jane Austen and the Military

to become. At the time Mr Price was a dashing lieutenant able to win his Frances' Ward's hand, there were 50 companies of marines with 100 men in each - a total of 5,000 men. These were headquartered at Portsmouth, Chatham and Plymouth, but nearly all the officers and men were at sea. By 1814 there were 31,400 marines.

Most of the larger ships in the Royal Navy had a detachment of marines on board. At this date, ships in the Royal Navy were "rated" with the biggest ships of 100 guns or more being First Rate ships, and each succeeding rate being smaller until the Sixth Rate of 20 to 28 guns. Smaller vessels - such as sloops, brigs or cutters - were not "ships" in naval parlance.

A Sixth Rate ship would have 23 marines, commanded by a marine lieutenant assisted by a sergeant and corporal. A First Rate might have had 104 marines, under the command of a captain with a lieutenant, a sergeant and two corporals.

The marines were originally raised as normal infantry battalions in the 1660s but very quickly were earmarked for naval cooperation. They were trained to find their way around ships, to make amphibious landings from rowing boats and to be expert at tackling all sorts of irregular combats that made them more light infantry than line infantry. It was in 1755 that they were transferred from the army to the navy.

It was because of their origin as army regiments that the marines wore red coats and white trousers. Indeed, it was their military heritage that meant that the marines had uniforms at all. Sailors in the Royal Navy did not wear uniforms of any kind until 1857. Up until then what the men wore was largely a matter for themselves, though some captains did lay down minimum requirements. Most captains made a point of paying for smart dress for the men who manned the boats as these were men who rowed the officers from one ship to another or around in port. The naval officers, of course, wore smart uniforms when on duty, but not the ratings.

This smart red and white uniform was a visual reminder of the

Jane Austen and the Military

non-sailor status of the marines. Indeed, the marines were nicknamed "lobsters" by the sailors as a result. The marines on board a ship slept in different cabins from the rest of the crew, and they ate their meals separately as well. The distinction between crew and marines was drawn clearly and with purpose.

Although the key official role of marines was to fight the enemy, an equally important function was to help the officers to maintain discipline on board. When a sailor was to be punished it was the marines who incarcerated him and prepared him for punishment. There was, at all times, a marine sentry on duty outside the door to the captain's cabin, and at other key points around the ship. The marines were an ever-present deterrent to unrest or even mutiny among the sailors.

In action, the marines used their muskets to shoot at the crews of any enemy ships that came close enough for those smooth bore weapons to be accurate - about 75 yards. Marines did not only fire from on deck, they would also climb up into the rigging and the crows nests so that they could fire down on to the enemy decks. The great Admiral Horatio Nelson was killed at the Battle of Trafalgar by a bullet fired by a French marine firing a musket from the rigging of the French warship Redoutable.

A painting showing the fall of Admiral Nelson [lying prostrate in the right foreground] at the Battle of Trafalgar in 1805. Note the number of marines present firing at the enemy ships with their muskets while the seamen work the cannon.

Being an officer of marines, like all positions in the military in a time of war, could be dangerous. We are not told how or when Mr Price was wounded, nor how serious his injuries were. Clearly they were bad enough for him to be retired from the marines on health grounds, but there is noticeable way in which his actions in the novel are hindered. He does not lack a limb, nor have trouble walking about

Jane Austen and the Military

town. Whatever his injuries were, they seem to have been of a remarkably non-visible kind.

At this date, officers who had retired through injury, ill health or old age were given a pension equivalent to half of whatever their salary would have been were they still active. For this reason being retired for whatever reason was known as "going on half pay".

Rates of pay were, rather unusually, made per lunar month, making them rather tricky to convert into modern concepts of annual salaries or weekly wages. A Captain of Marines would have been paid around £10 per lunar month - the precise sum depended on what sort of a ship he served. That would come out at perhaps £125 per year. The half pay that Mr Price would have been receiving depended to some

A painting showing the fall of Admiral Nelson [lying prostrate in the right foreground] at the Battle of Trafalgar in 1805. Note the number of marines present firing at the enemy ships with their muskets while the seamen work the cannon.

Jane Austen and the Military

extent on how many years he had been active at sea. In addition a man retired through injury could expect to receive additional allowances based on how badly crippled he was and whether or not this precluded him from getting other work. Mr Price does not seem to have been badly crippled. Perhaps he was getting something like £70 per year.

However much the Price family was receiving in terms of half pay it was not enough. Mrs Price therefore wrote to her estranged sisters asking for help. Her eldest sister, Maria, had married the wealthy Sir Thomas Bertram. The Bertrams offered to take in Fanny and raise her - which is how the novel's heroine comes to be living at Mansfield Park and to have all her various adventures that fill the novel.

There is not much else to be said about Mr Price's career. So far as Jane Austen tells us anything, it seems to be accurate and credible enough. But she does not tell us much at all.

Jane Austen and the Military

Chapter 6
Mr Weston and Military Status

(Emma)

We first meet Mr Weston in Chapter 1 of Emma when he marries Miss Anne Taylor, who for 16 years had been the governess of the eponymous Emma Woodhouse. Emma is feeling sorry for herself over the marriage since it means that her great friend, Miss Taylor, will no longer be living under the same roof as herself. Following Emma's train of thought, Jane Austen tells us:

"Mr. Weston was a man of unexceptionable character, easy fortune, suitable age, and pleasant manners; and there was some satisfaction in considering with what self-denying, generous friendship she had always wished and promoted the match; but it was a black morning's work for her."

A few pages later, Emma tells her father *"Mr. Weston is such a good-humoured, pleasant, excellent man, that he thoroughly deserves a good wife"*.

A neighbour, George Knightly, then visits and together the three of them discuss the marriage. We learn that Mr Weston is a widower, and has been so for some years and that most people in the village of Highbury believed that he would never marry again so great had been his love for his first wife.

It is not until Chapter 2 that we learn that Mr Weston was a military man in his youth. Austen opens the chapter thus:

"Mr. Weston was a native of Highbury, and born of a

Jane Austen and the Military

respectable family, which for the last two or three generations had been rising into gentility and property. He had received a good education, but, on succeeding early in life to a small independence, had become indisposed for any of the more homely pursuits in which his brothers were engaged, and had satisfied an active, cheerful mind and social temper by entering into the militia of his county, then embodied.

Captain Weston was a general favourite; and when the chances of his military life had introduced him to Miss Churchill, of a great Yorkshire family, and Miss Churchill fell in love with him, nobody was surprized, except her brother and his wife, who had never seen him, and who were full of pride and importance, which the connexion would offend.

Miss Churchill, however, being of age, and with the full command of her fortune—though her fortune bore no proportion to the family-estate—was not to be dissuaded from the marriage, and it took place, to the infinite mortification of Mr. and Mrs. Churchill, who threw her off with due decorum. It was an unsuitable connexion, and did not produce much happiness. Mrs. Weston ought to have found more in it, for she had a husband whose warm heart and sweet temper made him think every thing due to her in return for the great goodness of being in love with him; but though she had one sort of spirit, she had not the best. She had resolution enough to pursue her own will in spite of her brother, but not enough to refrain from unreasonable regrets at that brother's unreasonable anger, nor from missing the luxuries of her former home. They lived beyond their income, but still it was nothing in comparison of Enscombe: she did not cease to love her husband, but she wanted at once to be the wife of Captain Weston, and Miss Churchill of Enscombe.

Captain Weston, who had been considered, especially by the Churchills, as making such an amazing match, was proved

Jane Austen and the Military

to have much the worst of the bargain; for when his wife died, after a three years' marriage, he was rather a poorer man than at first, and with a child to maintain. From the expense of the child, however, he was soon relieved. The boy had, with the additional softening claim of a lingering illness of his mother's, been the means of a sort of reconciliation; and Mr. and Mrs. Churchill, having no children of their own, nor any other young creature of equal kindred to care for, offered to take the whole charge of the little Frank soon after her decease. Some scruples and some reluctance the widower-father may be supposed to

The title page of the first edition of Emma. Unlike Mansfield Park, this book did attract a good deal of attention and it sold well.

Jane Austen and the Military

have felt; but as they were overcome by other considerations, the child was given up to the care and the wealth of the Churchills, and he had only his own comfort to seek, and his own situation to improve as he could.

A complete change of life became desirable. He quitted the militia and engaged in trade, having brothers already established in a good way in London, which afforded him a favourable "opening. It was a concern which brought just employment enough. He had still a small house in Highbury, where most of his leisure days were spent; and between useful occupation and the pleasures of society, the next eighteen or twenty years of his life passed cheerfully away. He had, by that time, realised an easy competence—enough to secure the purchase of a little estate adjoining Highbury, which he had always longed for—enough to marry a woman as portionless even as Miss Taylor, and to live according to the wishes of his own friendly and social disposition."

This passage gives us about all we ever learn about Mr Weston's military past, but exposes a treasure trove of information on the social side of the military. So far we have met military men who have come from the upper end of the social scale, or who came from families with a military tradition. But Mr Weston comes from a very different sort of social background and his career is instructive.

Let us start with Mr Weston's social background. Austen tells us that "Mr. Weston was a native of Highbury, and born of a respectable family, which for the last two or three generations had been rising into gentility and property." Given that Mr Weston had been a widower for 20 years when the novel opens, and had been married to the first Mrs Weston for three years, his marriage must have taken place 23 years before the main action in the novel. Emma was published in 1816, so in 1793 or perhaps a little earlier.

The fictional Highbury is said to be in Surrey, 16 miles from London and 9 miles from Richmond. That would put it somewhere near where Long Ditton is today, but it is usually thought that Cobham

Jane Austen and the Military

or Leatherhead are more likely inspirations fro Highbury. They are further from both London or Richmond than the fictional village, but are more like it in description and were both visited by Austen.

At this date, the economy in Surrey was not doing very well. From about 1780 onwards the Industrial Revolution was transforming the British economy. New factories in rapidly growing cities were creating new jobs, new trades and new wealth for all classes of society. And the concurrent Agricultural Revolution was leading to a boom in farming output and food processing that was fuelling a similar, if less spectacular, growth in rural jobs and incomes.

But Surrey was missing out on both. Its poor soils created non-productive sandy heaths in the northwest of the county, chalk uplands fit only for sheep grazing in the centre and boggy clay soils covered in forests to the south. The high chalk downs made transport difficult, something made no better by the lack of navigable rivers. It was a bit of a rural backwater, enlivened only by army units on manoeuvres on the sandy heaths and naval couriers galloping up and down the London to Portsmouth Road.

The general lack of economic progress in Surrey is reflected in its population figures. While the UK as a whole had 12.1 million inhabitants in 1811, Surrey had barely over 100,000. That excludes the densely built up areas just south of London Bridge that lay within the Surrey boundaries, but were really part of booming London. The county was sparsely populated and those who lived there were generally doing badly and frequently poverty stricken.

So the Weston family in which Mr Weston grew up would have been something unusual in Surrey in the 1780s and 1790s. They were, we are told by Austen, "a respectable family, which for the last two or three generations had been rising into gentility and property." Such prosperity would have been rather unusual in Surrey towards the end of the 18th century. We learn that the two other Weston brothers ran a business in London, which no doubt accounts for their growing wealth.

Jane Austen and the Military

But our Mr Weston "on succeeding early in life to a small independence, had become indisposed for any of the more homely pursuits in which his brothers were engaged, and had satisfied an active, cheerful mind and social temper by entering into the militia of his county, then embodied."

Quite what a "small independence" might mean is not stated here, but from other works by Austen we can conclude that she means an income based on land rents or investments that might be between £200 and £500 per year. This would be enough to free Mr Weston from the arduous business of actually working for a living, but would not have been enough to make him a really good marriage prospect - at least in the social milieu in which Austen lived. Where this independent income came from is not stated, but presumably it was settled on him by his father, as would have been normal at this time.

Since we know that the Weston family were natives of Surrey the "militia of his county" can only mean the Surrey Militia. This body of troops was formed 1757 and within two years had grown so large that it was reformed into two separate battalions. It is likely that these large number of recruits came from the urban northeast of the county, which had packed into its few hundred acres more than four times as many people as the rest of the county combined.

We know that Mr Weston's first marriage took place in 1793 and that he was a captain at that point. Assuming that he had had no military experience before joining the part time militia it is unlikely that a man from a background in trade would have taken precedence over a militia officer from a landed background. Perhaps he joined as a lieutenant and then gained promotion to captain when he warranted it.

The pay of a captain in the militia was £193 per year, which added to the "small independence" that Mr Weston already had would have given him a tidy but not very high income. We are told that his first wife, Miss Churchill, came from "a great Yorkshire family" but that her own inheritance "bore no proportion to the family-estate" - in

Jane Austen and the Military

other words it was quite small and may have been on a par with that of her new husband.

So far so good as regards Mr Weston's military career. In the later 1780s and early 1790s the militia was still a part time affair. The officers and men would muster in the spring and spend a few summer weeks practising drills and manoeuvres before disbanding again before the harvest needed to be brought in. Often the militia would march to another county to take part in joint manoeuvres with another

An illustration from a 19th Century edition of the book shows Captain Weston hurrying with two umbrellas to the rescue of Emma and Miss Taylor, thus showing his good manners and gentlemanly status.

Jane Austen and the Military

regiment. When Britain joined the war against Revolutionary France these joint manoeuvres were carried out on an ever greater scale. No doubt it was during one of these that Mr Weston met Miss Churchill of Yorkshire. Presumably the Surrey Militia went to Yorkshire for a few weeks.

It is interesting that Austen seems to imply that the young Captain Weston was working full time with the militia. Back in the 1780s and early 1790s this would have been very unusual. The vast majority of militia officers turned out for the summer manoeuvres, but otherwise stuck to their civilian lives. Only a very few spent any other time in the militia. There would have been a small depot staff that was responsible for the purchase and storage of uniforms, weapons, ammunition and the like. These men were not, as a rule, officers in the militia regiment but civilian staff employed by the Lord Lieutenant of the county.

It is, therefore, difficult to see what Captain Weston was doing working full time in the militia.

However, by the time that Austen was writing the militia had been embodied full time in response to the threat of invasion by Napoleonic France. We have already me Wickham from Pride and Prejudice who was a full time militia officer. It is possible that in her treatment of Captain Weston, Austen is making an error. She may have assumed that what was the case in her day had been the case all those years earlier when, in fact, it had not.

In any case, Austen is quite correct when she says that Weston "quitted the militia and engaged in trade". Militia officers were not obliged to stay in the militia if they did not want to do so. They could leave at short notice, and many did exactly that.

That young Captain Weston left the militia to enter into business would have had important social implications for Austen's readers. This would undoubtedly have been seen as a step down in social rank for young Weston, albeit a no doubt healthy step up as regards his income. Officers in His Majesty's armed forces - even those in the

Jane Austen and the Military

militia - were entitled to be considered as gentlemen. A man working in trade could not be considered to be a gentleman. That young Weston felt able to make this move without much of a qualm would have spoken volumes to Austen's readers.

Looking back on Mr Weston's military career we can see that Austen has not told us very much. Most of what she does share with us is done so to make implications about his social status and background. What she tells us is accurate enough, with the exception of Austen seeming to think that the militia was a full time force in the later 1780s when it was not. So here she has been reasonably accurate, but not completely so.

Chapter 7

Frederick Wentworth and prize money

(Persuasion)

With Captain Frederick Wentworth we encounter an aspect of warfare that has, at least officially, disappeared entirely: the ability to become very rich out of defeating the enemy. There has always been some degree of theft and robbery in warfare, and there still is, but during the Napoleonic Wars the looting of the enemy was turned in a large scale and highly profitable business by the Royal Navy under the term "Prize Money". But before dealing with that system directly, let us see what Jane Austen has to tell us on the subject in her novel *Persuasion* when talking about the naval officer Captain Frederick Wentworth.

We first meet Frederick Wentworth at the opening of Chapter 2 when he is introduced as the younger brother of Mr Wentworth, the curate of Monkford in Somerset. Austen relates:

"He was not Mr Wentworth, the former curate of Monkford, however suspicious appearances may be, but a Captain Frederick Wentworth, his brother, who being made commander in consequence of the action off St Domingo, and not immediately employed, had come into Somersetshire, in the summer of 1806; and having no parent living, found a home for half a year at Monkford. He was, at that time, a remarkably fine young man, with a great deal of intelligence, spirit, and brilliancy; and Anne an extremely pretty girl, with gentleness,

Jane Austen and the Military

modesty, taste, and feeling. Half the sum of attraction, on either side, might have been enough, for he had nothing to do, and she had hardly anybody to love; but the encounter of such lavish recommendations could not fail. They were gradually acquainted, and when acquainted, rapidly and deeply in love. It would be difficult to say which had seen highest perfection in the other, or which had been the happiest: she, in receiving his declarations and proposals, or he in having them accepted.

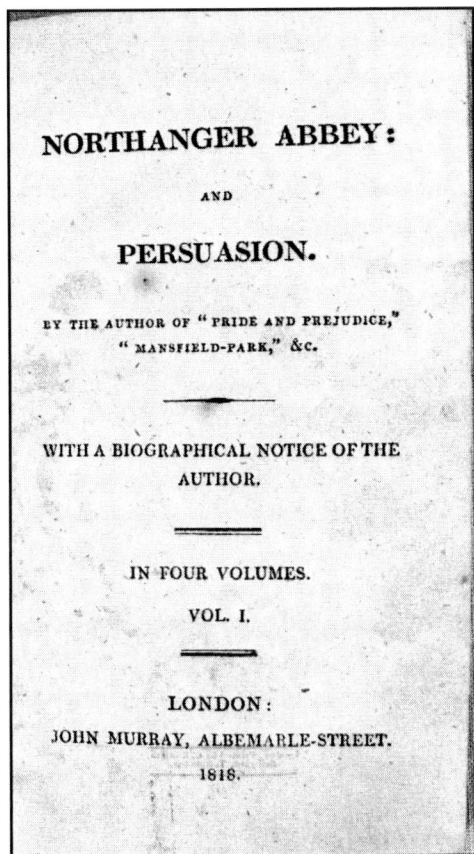

The title page of Northanger Abbey and Persuasion. The two books were published together after Austen's death.

Jane Austen and the Military

A short period of exquisite felicity followed, and but a short one. Troubles soon arose. Sir Walter, on being applied to, without actually withholding his consent, or saying it should never be, gave it all the negative of great astonishment, great coldness, great silence, and a professed resolution of doing nothing for his daughter. He thought it a very degrading alliance; and Lady Russell, though with more tempered and pardonable pride, received it as a most unfortunate one.

Anne Elliot, with all her claims of birth, beauty, and mind, to throw herself away at nineteen; involve herself at nineteen in an engagement with a young man, who had nothing but himself to recommend him, and no hopes of attaining affluence, but in the chances of a most uncertain profession, and no connexions to secure even his farther rise in the profession, would be, indeed, a throwing away, which she grieved to think of! Anne Elliot, so young known to so few, to be snatched off by a stranger without alliance or fortune; or rather sunk by him into a state of most wearing, anxious, youth-killing dependence! It must not be, if by any fair interference of friendship, any representations from one who had almost a mother's love, and mother's rights, it would be prevented.

Captain Wentworth had no fortune. He had been lucky in his profession; but spending freely, what had come freely, had realized nothing. But he was confident that he should soon be rich: full of life and ardour, he knew that he should soon have a ship, and soon be on a station that would lead to everything he wanted. He had always been lucky; he knew he should be so still. Such confidence, powerful in its own warmth, and bewitching in the wit which often expressed it, must have been enough for Anne; but Lady Russell saw it very differently."

Perhaps inevitably, Lady Russell and other members of the Elliot family step in and break up the romance. Wentworth went back to sea, Anne lived a lively but unmarried life in Somerset.

Jane Austen and the Military

So, Austen tells us, that back in 1806 "Captain Frederick Wentworth" was a "commander". Here at once we are in danger of heading into some confusion. Strictly speaking it was impossible for a man in 1806 to hold the rank of Captain and Commander at one and the same time. Strictly speaking a Captain - or more properly a Post-Captain was the commander of a ship in the Royal Navy. Smaller vessels - such as sloops, brigs and cutters were commanded by officers of a lesser rank. The smaller such ships were commanded by lieutenants, the larger ones by men who held the rank of Commander. However, the officer in charge of a vessel of any size in the Royal Navy was addressed as "Captain" by his crew when on board and as "Captain of the [name of craft] when ashore. Thus the "Captain" element of Wentworth's title is merely a courtesy or honorific. His actual title in 1806 was Commander.

Next we come to what Austen calls "the action off St Domingo". This is better known to history as the Battle of San Domingo and was fought on 6 February 1806. It turned out to be the last major fleet action of the Napoleonic Wars. As such it would have been well known to Austen's original readers, though few people today other than naval historians are familiar with it.

The battle was doubly well-known to Jane Austen because her brother Sir Francis Austen fought in the battle. At the time he was commander of the 74-gun Third Rate warship HMS Canopus.

In December 1805 Vice-Admiral Corentin-Urbain Leissègues left France with orders to attack British merchant ships and convoys in the North Atlantic to disrupt British trade. This would, in turn, disrupt the tax money flowing into the British government and - so Napoleon hoped - hinder its ability to wage war effectively. However, a storm struck Leissègues fleet and he put into the island of San Domingo for repairs. He considered himself safe as no British fleet was stationed in the area.

However, the British Admiral John Duckworth was having problems of his own. He was supposed to be cruising off Cadiz to

Jane Austen and the Military

stop that port being used by French ships - Spain at this date being an ally of France. But on 23 December 1805 a British frigate, HMS Arethusa, sought him out to report that a group of French ships was cruising to the north of the Canary Islands. Duckworth, acting without orders, abandoned his station and set off to investigate.

He found the French ships previously encountered by the Arethusa. They turned out to be six ships of the line with two frigates and two brigs under the command of Admiral Jean-Baptiste Willaumez. Willaumez was heading for the South Atlantic and Indian Ocean on a raiding cruise of his own. Duckworth gave chase, but the French ships kept ahead of him. For over 36 hours the pursuit continued, not ending until both fleets were far out into the Atlantic.

After giving up this chase, Duckworth decided to continue across the Atlantic to Barbados to pick up supplies that were badly needed by his ships after weeks cruising off Cadiz. While Duckworth was provisioning his ships a sloop, the Kingfisher, came in to report that three French ships of the line had been sighted off San Domingo. The report would turn out to be erroneous. Leissègues had with him five ships of the line, two frigates and a corvette. But with seven ships of the line, two frigates and two brigs, Duckworth believed that he heavily outnumbered this new French squadron. He at once put to sea and headed for San Domingo where Leissègues had no idea that a battle was in the offing.

Just after dawn on 6 February Duckworth came within sight of San Domingo. His lookout reported two French frigates putting to sea while five ships of the line and other craft remained in port. Duckworth ordered his ships to crowd on sail to achieve more speed and to attack at once.

Leissègues was on shore when the British ships came in sight. He hurriedly gave orders for his fleet to get to sea and, rather ignominiously, had to be ferried out to his flagship in a fast schooner as she headed west. The French formed up into a conventional line of battle with the big warships following each other in a line. This

Jane Austen and the Military

would allow them all to fire their broadsides at the same target simultaneously and was the usual way that an admiral would position his larger vessels for a battle. His flagship, the massive Imperial of 120 guns, was second in the line.

Duckworth, meanwhile, divided his fleet into two squadrons. One was to race on and try to get ahead of the French, while the other would close up on the French from behind. Duckworth thus hoped to get the French trapped between two fires. None of ships mounted more than 74 guns so although he had more ships, he actually had fewer guns than the French he was so keen to attack.

The battle began a little after 10am as Duckworth's forward squadron caught up with the front of the French line. By concentrating on the lead ship, the Alexandre, the British managed to disrupt the neat French line, while the presence of the coast close by stopped the

The Battle of San Domengo by Thomas Horbrook. In this painting HMS Canopus, which was commanded in the battle by Jane Austen's brother Francis is shown on the far right hurrying up to join the rather disorganised running fight.

Jane Austen and the Military

French from regrouping. Both Alexandre and Imperial turned off their course to try to manoeuvre so that they could rake one or more of the British ships.

To rake an enemy ship was the hope of every naval commander. It meant to position your ship either at the bows or stern of the enemy vessel so that your entire broadside of guns could fire at him while his could not fire at yours. The devastation that a raking broadside could inflict was made all the worse by the fact that the timbers of a warship were thinner at the bows and stern, meaning that more cannonballs would smash their way into the interior to kill men and overturn guns.

The British captains were, however, aware of the danger and themselves engaged in a series of twists and turns both to evade the French and to get their own guns to bear. As the lead ships snaked around each other they became gradually hidden in great billowing clouds of gun smoke.

Meanwhile, at the rear of the French line, Duckworth's second squadron got into action around 10.40am. The French ships were already in disarray as they sought to avoid getting sucked into the developing battle ahead of them and so found themselves outmanoeuvred by the British. First one, then another French ship surrendered after taking heavy punishment.

By 11.30am the three rear French ships had surrendered and the rearward British squadron plunged into the melee ahead of them. They went in to quickly and two ships collided in the smoke, one losing its bowsprit and then drifting damaged out of the battle. So dense had the smoke become that none of the captains were entirely certain where they were, nor where the other ships might be found. At 11.45am the French flagship, Imperial, hit a coral reef, all her masts going over the side with the force of the impact. A few minutes later Alexandre followed. Their crews soon realised that both ships had been badly holed below the waterline, but they were not sinking as they were stuck on the reef.

Jane Austen and the Military

Suddenly realising that they were in danger of being wrecked themselves, the British captains scrambled to get their ships away from the dangerous reef. Every British ship was damaged, with most having lost at least part of a mast or spar which hindered their ability to manoeuvre. Not wanting to risk ending up on the reef, Duckworth pulled back.

While the British hastened to make temporary repairs, the French took advantage of the lull to ferry their stranded crews ashore in rowing boats. It was not until two days later that Duckworth felt confident enough to approach the reef. By then most of the Frenchmen had escaped. Nevertheless, he sent men over in boats to take prisoner the few men left and seize anything of value that could easily be gotten off the French ships. Duckworth then had the stranded French ships set on fire so that the French would be unable to salvage anything from them.

The victory made the Atlantic Ocean safe for British merchantmen. Everyone in the British fleet benefitted - and it is to this that Austen is alluding when she says that young Wentworth was "made commander in consequence of the action off St Domingo".

One British captain was knighted, another made a baronet. All the junior officers were promoted by one rung up the ladder. Rather ironically the only man not to benefit in terms of title or promotion was Admiral Duckworth himself. He had, it must be remembered, left Cadiz without orders and so had allowed a good deal of French and Spanish shipping to use that port while he was away. There were some naval officers who thought that he was lucky to get away without being court martialled.

Titles and promotions apart, there were also more solid rewards in the form of hard cash. And Duckworth did get his due share of these.

Money paid out for the victory at San Domingo, and for all naval successes, took two forms. First there was "Head Money". This was a cash sum of £5 paid out for every enemy crew member who was

Jane Austen and the Military

killed, wounded or captured. It was easy enough to work out enemy casualties for a ship that was sunk or captured, but working out the enemy's casualties was an inexact science, for it was quite impossible to know how many enemy crew had been killed on a ship that managed to evade capture. In the event it was usual for the Admiralty to make an informed guess.

For the Battle of San Domingo the Admiralty guessed that around 2,000 French sailors had been killed or captured. But when the matter was debated in the House of Commons, the MPs were so delighted with the victory that they voted to change the Admiralty report so that the official figure became instead 4,268. This was a way of ensuring that the British crews got a higher cash reward than they would otherwise have done.

In addition to Head Money, there was also "Prize Money". Originally this had been a way to split up between the crew the cash value of anything that they captured. Not only naval crews, but also pirates, privateers and buccaneers used this system. Any ships, cargoes or other materials that were captured were taken to a convenient nearby port and auctioned off. The money gained was then divided up among the officers and crew according to a previously agreed system.

By the time of the Battle of San Domingo, however, the Royal Navy had formalised this ad hoc system. Every port where Britain had a formal presence had to institute a "Prize Court". Wherever possible this was composed of senior naval officers, but in more remote parts of the globe the British ambassador or consul might himself act as the Prize Court.

Any ships, cargoes or other materials captured by a naval ship had to be taken to a nearby Prize Court at the first opportunity. The Court had to make a number of decisions. The first was to ensure that the capture had been made according to the rules of war and that the thing captured did, indeed, belong to an enemy government, company or national.

Jane Austen and the Military

Next the Prize Court had to decide how much prize money would be paid. For merchant ships and their cargoes the easiest way to do this was to have the items auctioned off at the first convenient opportunity.

For enemy warships this was not possible. Instead the Prize Court would decide if the captured ship was going to be useful to the Royal Navy or not. If it was deemed to be of no use to the Royal Navy, it was broken up and the various bits of timber, nails, ropes and so forth sold as scrap.

On the other hand if the ship was bought by the Royal Navy the Prize Court had to decide how much to pay. There was by 1806 a set list of purchase prices for warships. A schooner would be bought for £1,370, a frigate for £8,200, a 74-gun ship of the line for £43,322, an 80-gun ship of the line for £53,458 and a 100-gun ship of the line for £67,458. From these prices would be deducted whatever it cost the Royal Navy to repair the damaged enemy warship and get it into a fit state to go to sea.

This system had a marked effect on how battles were fought at sea. Naval crews knew that they stood to make a lot of money if they could capture enemy ships, but very little if the enemy ship were to be sunk. For this reason it was unusual for a Royal Navy ship to blast an enemy with it heavy cannon until it sank. It was much more usual for the heavy guns to be used to inflict just enough damage to cripple the enemy vessel, then grapeshot would be used to kill as many of the enemy crew as possible before the two ships were brought together.

The British crew would then swarm aboard the enemy ship armed with cutlasses, pistols and pikes in an effort to kill so many of the enemy crew that the captain - or the most senior surviving officer - surrendered. Hopefully very little damage had been done to the fabric of the captured ship.

Once the total amount of cash available had been added up from Head Money and Prize Money, it was time to divide it up. Once again,

Jane Austen and the Military

the Royal Navy had by 1806 drawn up strict rules about how this should be done.

First, those eligible to a share of the money was defined as being the crews of all ships that had been within sight of the action when the enemy surrendered - whether or not they had been involved in the actual fighting. The reasoning behind this was that the decision by an enemy captain to surrender might be influenced by the fact that other British ships were coming to join a battle, even if they had not yet done so. For the purpose of Prize Money, the meaning of "in sight" was stretched somewhat. It basically meant any ship that would have been in sight if it were not for all the gun smoke billowing around.

One person who had not been present at the battle was eligible to a share of Prize Money. That was the flag officer in overall command of the area of sea where the battle took place. Very often, of course, the admiral was at a large battle but for smaller action she was usually not actually present. The rationale for giving the commanding admiral or commodore a share was that it had been his decision to send the ships to the place where they made the capture and so deserved some reward for his astute decisions.

Once the long and complicated tasks of deciding how much cash was to be shared out and who was eligible to a share, the just as demanding task of doing the dividing of cash could begin. At the time of the Battle of San Domingo the standard way to divide up Head and Prize Money was as follows:

1/8th was given to the Flag Officer;

1/4th was divided among all the captains of eligible ships;

1/8th was divided among all the other officers of eligible ships;

1/8th was divided among the senior warrant officers, surgeons, chaplains, Royal Marine officers and secretaries of the eligible ships;

1/8th was divided among the midshipmen, junior warrant officers, masters mates and Marine non-commissioned officers;

1/4th was divided among the remaining crew members of eligible ships.

Jane Austen and the Military

This was a complicated system and on occasion it could take many months for all the sums to be done and the money paid over. Nevertheless the rewards could be enormous. The highest recorded payout of Prize Money came in 1762 when the Spanish treasure ship Hermione was captured by two British ships. The British captains got £65,000 each, while even the lowest ranking sailor was given £485.

The rewards paid out for the Battle of San Domingo were nothing like this large - the two largest French ships had been wrecked and so did not go to a Prize Court - but nonetheless were substantial. Not that this did the young Wentworth much good. As Austen tells us:

"Captain Wentworth had no fortune. He had been lucky in his profession; but spending freely, what had come freely, had realized nothing." In other words, whatever prize money he had got, from his time as a lieutenant he had already spent. Well, he was a young man after all.

Nevertheless, he had been promoted to be Commander. It is clear that he was in Somerset while he waited for a ship to become available. As soon as one did, he was off.

We learn later in Chapter 8 that his first command had been HMS Asp. Wentworth describes it like this in a conversation with Anne Elliott. Anne, along with Louisa and Henrietta Musgrove, have got out a copy of the Navy List - a book which lists all the ships in the Royal Navy. The first speaker in this section is Anne.

"Your first was the Asp, I remember; we will look for the Asp."

"You will not find her there. Quite worn out and broken up. I was the last man who commanded her. Hardly fit for service then. Reported fit for home service for a year or two, and so I was sent off to the West Indies."

The girls looked all amazement.

"The Admiralty," he continued, *"entertain themselves now and then, with sending a few hundred men to sea, in a ship not fit to be employed. But they have a great many to provide for;*

Jane Austen and the Military

and among the thousands that may just as well go to the bottom as not, it is impossible for them to distinguish the very set who may be least missed."

It might be suspected that Wentworth was exaggerating the bad condition of HMS Asp to try to get some sympathy from the young ladies, but that apart, how accurate is Austen here?

A long-barrelled 24 pounder gun mounted on a naval carriage although now preserved in a coastal fort. These were long range weapons, but were heavy for a small craft to carry with safety. [Photo Paul Hermans]

Jane Austen and the Military

Assuming that she means that the Asp was the ship that Wentworth took command of when he left Somerset in 1806, then there was no ship named HMS Asp in 1806 that by 1816 was no longer on the Navy List. There were, however, two ships named HMS Asp that were active during the Napoleonic Wars. Did Austen have one of these in mind?

The first HMS Asp was a gun brig that was built in 1797 at Rotherhithe by the shipwright John Randall. She was one of 15 identical brigs built in 1797 by a variety of makers. She was 158 feet long and 22 feet wide with a shallow draft. She had a crew of 60 men. As a brig she had two tall masts with square-rigged sails, which made her very fast and easy to manoeuvre.

The armament of these ships was most unusual, and was designed for a specific purpose. Pointing forward over the bows was a pair of long-barrelled 24 pounder guns. These were long-range weapons which were able to throw a cannonball a distance of 1,200 yards with accuracy. Its maximum range was well over a mile, though not even an experienced gunner could hit a ship at that range with any certainty. These were big, heavy weapons that were usually put on board the larger frigates and were quite out sized for a brig.

The other ten guns on the Asp were 18 pounder carronades, mounted nine either side to fire as broadsides. These were new weapons in 1797, having been invented only ten years earlier. It was a very different sort of weapon to the long barrelled 24 pounder.

A carronade was a short-range weapon that was cheap to make and easy to use, requiring a smaller crew than the heavier cannon. Carronades had a short barrel, but one of a very wide calibre. They could throw a solid cannonball perhaps 600 yards with some attempt at accuracy, but were truly deadly when loaded with grapeshot - that is a canvas bag filled with small iron balls, each weighing around 8 ounces or so. A bag of grapeshot might hold as many as 36 balls. When fired, the balls sprayed out rather like a gigantic sawn off shotgun, with horrific results to any men who were in the way.

Jane Austen and the Military

This peculiar armament was suited to the purpose of these gun brigs. They were designed to operate in the coastal waters around Britain, protecting ports or escorting convoys. They would also be sent across the English Channel to attack French ports and French convoys. Their long-range bow guns enabled them to shoot at an enemy ship while chasing it in the hope of inflicting some damage and slowing it down. Once an enemy ship had been caught, the brig would seek to get in close to use its devastating carronades to butcher the enemy crew, and so allow the enemy ship to be captured relatively intact. This was, of course, important when it came to getting prize money.

After reporting that he was sent out to the West Indies in the Asp, Wentworth continues "Ah! she was a dear old Asp to me. She did all that I wanted. I knew she would. I knew that we should either go to the bottom together, or that she would be the making of me; and I never had two days of foul weather all the time I was at sea in her; and after taking privateers enough to be very entertaining, I had the good luck in my passage home the next autumn..."

So here Austen is both correct and incorrect in how she reports these gun brigs being used. She is correct that they were used primarily to hunt down privateers [privately owned warships used to attack enemy merchant ships] and the like, but quite incorrect to say that these ships went across the Atlantic. They were designed for coastal use and that is where they stayed.

The vulnerability of the gun brigs in the open sea is starkly revealed by the fate of the Crash, a sister ship to the Asp. On 23 August 1799 she was returning to Britain from the Netherlands across the southern part of the North Sea when a storm came on. The Crash proved to be quite incapable of coping with the high waves. On the second day of the storm her commander, Lieutenant Bulkeley Mackworth Praed, ordered his crew to throw the guns overboard to lighten the ship and make her ride higher in the water. It did little good, the masts were damaged and rigging torn away by the storm.

Jane Austen and the Military

On 26 August she was driven ashore and wrecked on Vlieland, one of the Frisian Islands off the Dutch coast. Another of the gun brigs, the Contest, was similarly wrecked in the same storm.

It was because of this vulnerability to bad weather that the commanders of gun brigs were ordered to strictly remain in coastal waters. That made them somewhat less use in the war than had been intended and so all but one of them were sold by the Royal Navy between 1799 and 1805.

It is possible that Austen was misled by the sale of these craft. She may have concluded that the Asp had been a rotten old vessel that was fit only for scrap. In fact these vessels were sound and good quality craft that were sold only because they had proved to be

A short barrelled carronade. These weapons were devastatingly effective at short range, but hopelessly inaccurate at longer ranges. Note that the gun is mounted on a sliding wooden base rather than on wheels. This made it quicker to reload and return to the side of the ship to be fired again. [Photo Bjenks].

Jane Austen and the Military

unsuitable for the purposes that the Royal Navy wanted to use them. Once sold they all went on to have long and profitable careers as coastal trading craft.

The other HMS Asp of the Napoleonic Wars was a French sloop that had been built in 1806 as the Rivoli. She was armed with fourteen 24 pounder carronades, again an armament designed to fight other small craft at close range. As a sloop, however, she was an ocean-going craft intended for international service. In July 1808 the Rivoli had the misfortune to run into the much larger British frigate HMS Acasta off the cost of Venezuela. After a short, but vicious battle, the French commander Ensign Lamanon surrendered.

The Rivoli was quickly bought by the Royal Navy and repaired ready to re-enter service. She was renamed the Asp, presumably because the Admiralty felt it better to name a warship after a venomous snake than an Italian holiday resort. She remained on the American side of the Atlantic for some years and took part in a number of small actions.

In 1810 she was sent back across the Atlantic to carry despatches from Admiral Sir Alexander Cochrane to the Admiralty. When she arrived in Portsmouth the authorities there decided to pay off her crew and put the ship "into ordinary". This meant that she was put into reserve. She was taken to a quiet corner of Portsmouth Harbour where he masts, sails, rigging and guns were removed for storage ashore. She was then given a tiny crew of half a dozen men under a warrant officer in order to keep the bilge pumps going, touch up flaking paint and generally keep the hull in good condition. We do not know the reason why this potentially useful naval ship was laid up in time of warfare, but it might be that she was in not very good condition.

That she could not have been in very bad condition is shown by the fact that when peace came the Royal Navy sold her for £1,050. She was bought by John Bell, who converted her into a whaler and sent her off to the Pacific. As a whaler she undertook five successful and highly profitable voyages, but she was lost on rocks off

Jane Austen and the Military

Madagascar on her sixth voyage - all the crew being saved.

At one point, Austen has Admiral Croft say of the Asp:

""Phoo! phoo!" cried the Admiral, "what stuff these young fellows talk! Never was a better sloop than the Asp in her day. For an old built sloop, you would not see her equal. Lucky fellow to get her! He knows there must have been twenty better men than himself applying for her at the same time. Lucky fellow to get anything so soon, with no more interest than his."

That might seem to settle the matter. Austen meant the second Asp, the captured French sloop.

However, one throwaway line by Austen indicates that while she may have been inspired by one or other of these Asps, the ship commanded by Wentworth was something quite different. Austen has Wentworth tell the young ladies next that:

"I had the good luck in my passage home the next autumn, to fall in with the very French frigate I wanted. I brought her into Plymouth; and here another instance of luck. We had not been six hours in the Sound, when a gale came on, which lasted four days and nights, and which would have done for poor old Asp in half the time; our touch with the Great Nation not having much improved our condition. Four-and-twenty hours later, and I should only have been a gallant Captain Wentworth, in a small paragraph at one corner of the newspapers; and being lost in only a sloop, nobody would have thought about me." Anne's shudderings were to herself alone; but the Miss Musgroves could be as open as they were sincere, in their exclamations of pity and horror."

It is clear that Wentworth captured the French frigate in battle. This would have been quite impossible for a small craft such as a brig or sloop. So Wentworth's Asp must have been at the very least a small frigate, possibly something rather larger. And here we run into some real difficulties regarding Austen's version of Wentworth's career.

When he left Somerset in 1806 to take up his first command he

Jane Austen and the Military

had the rank of Commander. That entitled him to command a small vessel, such as a brig or sloop that we know the real Asps to have been. However, a frigate was an altogether bigger, more important and more expensive ship. The Admiralty was not in the habit of entrusting such a craft to a mere Commander - especially not one who was without influence, connections or massive experience as we know Wentworth to have been in 1806. This was, instead, the job for a man who had been promoted to the rank of Captain.

Clearly Austen has got muddled here. Either Wentworth was a Commander or he was a Captain, he cannot have been both. Either the Asp was a sloop or a frigate. The puzzle cannot be sorted out, so Austen must have been in error somehow.

Moving Wentworth's career forward, we learn that his next ship was HMS Laconia. As the conversation between the young ladies holding their copy of the Navy List and Wentworth continues, Austen tells us:

"The girls were now hunting for the Laconia; and Captain Wentworth could not deny himself the pleasure of taking the precious volume into his own hands to save them the trouble, and once more read aloud the little statement of her name and rate, and present non-commissioned class, observing over it that she too had been one of the best friends man ever had.

"Ah! those were pleasant days when I had the Laconia! How fast I made money in her. A friend of mine and I had such a lovely cruise together off the Western Islands. Poor Harville, sister! You know how much he wanted money: worse than myself. He had a wife. Excellent fellow. I shall never forget his happiness. He felt it all, so much for her sake. I wished for him again the next summer, when I had still the same luck in the Mediterranean."

"And I am sure, Sir," said Mrs Musgrove, "it was a lucky day for us, when you were put captain into that ship. We shall never forget what you did."

Jane Austen and the Military

This little exchange tells us that Wentworth made his great fortune of £25,000 in prize money chiefly with the Laconia. She was beyond doubt a frigate and as such would have been sent roving around the oceans to snap up French merchant ships as fast as she could. In this Austen is quite correct. Command of a frigate in the Caribbean and Mediterranean was exactly how a young naval officer would become wealthy.

Much later in Chapter 23 Wentworth is again talking to Anne. Finding that they still love each other after their years of separation he says "Tell me if, when I returned to England in the year eight, with a few thousand pounds, and was posted into the Laconia, if I had then written to you, would you have answered my letter? Would you, in short, have renewed the engagement then?"

This tells us that it was in 1808 that he was promoted out of the Asp and into the Laconia. The latter was undoubtedly a frigate and to command her he must have been a Captain. This is only two years after he was promoted from lieutenant to be a commander and given command of the Asp. That is a remarkably swift promotion even for a young man of considerable talents - as we must suppose Wentworth to have been.

The feeling is inescapable that Austen has got herself a bit muddled up here over Wentworth's career for the purposes of the storyline. The interlude between the engagement between Anne and Wentworth being broken off and it being renewed could not be very long, otherwise Anne would have been rather too old to be a bewitching young heroine of marriageable age in the Austen style.

Considerations of age do not affect prospective husbands in the same way, but even so Wentworth had to be young and penniless at the time of the earlier engagement to be deemed to be unsuitable by Anne's family. So his career path from penniless youngster to mature man of means had to get compressed. Unfortunately this was done at the expense of accuracy when it came to ranks and ships in the Royal Navy.

Jane Austen and the Military

It is also worth noting that in this exchange we get introduced not only to the Laconia, but also the subject of "Rates". It is time to turn to Captain James Benwick.

But before we leave the puzzles of HMS Asp, it is worth remarking that Jane Austen may have had a very personal reason for giving this name to the first ship commanded by her fictional Captain Wentworth. He own brother Sir Francis Austen was a naval officer and his first command had been HMS Cleopatra. That ship had been named for the famous ancient Egyptian queen, Cleopatra VII, who had been the lover of both Julius Caesar and Mark Antony as well as being a powerful monarch in her own right. After her final defeat by Augustus, she chose to commit suicide - and did so by allowing herself to be bitten by a venomous snake - an asp!

HMS Cleopatra, the ship commanded by Austen's brother Sir Franis Austen. It is likely that this frigate served as the real life template for the fictional Asp.

Chapter 8
James Benwick and the Rating of Naval Ships
(Persuasion)

Captain James Benwick features in Persuasion, where he is a friend of Captain and Mrs Harville, having previously been engaged to Captain Harville's sister Frances before her untimely death before the novel begins. He also, along with Harville, had served with Captain Wentworth earlier in his career.

We meet Benwick in Chapter 11 when Captain Wentworth, Anne and others are on a visit to Lyme Regis, Dorset. Wentworth goes to call on his old friend, Captain Harville. Austen takes up the story:

"Captain Benwick had some time ago been first lieutenant of the Laconia; and the account which Captain Wentworth had given of him, on his return from Lyme before, his warm praise of him as an excellent young man and an officer, whom he had always valued highly, which must have stamped him well in the esteem of every listener, had been followed by a little history of his private life, which rendered him perfectly interesting in the eyes of all the ladies. He had been engaged to Captain Harville's sister, and was now mourning her loss. They had been a year or two waiting for fortune and promotion. Fortune came, his prize-money as lieutenant being great; promotion, too, came at last; but Fanny Harville did not live to know it. She had died the preceding summer while he was at sea. Captain Wentworth believed it impossible for man to be more

Jane Austen and the Military

attached to woman than poor Benwick had been to Fanny Harville, or to be more deeply afflicted under the dreadful change. He considered his disposition as of the sort which must suffer heavily, uniting very strong feelings with quiet, serious, and retiring manners, and a decided taste "for reading, and sedentary pursuits. To finish the interest of the story, the friendship between him and the Harvilles seemed, if possible, augmented by the event which closed all their views of alliance, and Captain Benwick was now living with them entirely. Captain Harville had taken his present house for half a year; his taste, and his health, and his fortune, all directing him to a residence inexpensive, and by the sea; and the grandeur of the country, and the retirement of Lyme in the winter, appeared exactly adapted to Captain Benwick's state of mind. The sympathy and good-will excited towards Captain Benwick was very great."

She continues:

"Captain Harville was a tall, dark man, with a sensible, benevolent countenance; a little lame; and from strong features and want of health, looking much older than Captain Wentworth. Captain Benwick looked, and was, the youngest of the three, and, compared with either of them, a little man. He had a pleasing face and a melancholy air, just as he ought to have, and drew back from conversation."

This is about all we learn about Benwick's naval career - and we learn even less about Harville's - but it is enough to shed some light on the matter of the types of ship in the Royal Navy. We already know from the references Austen makes to Wentworth that HMS Laconia had "a name and rate", and now we learn that she had a first lieutenant - and by implication at least a second lieutenant if not more.

There was no such ship as the HMS Laconia in the Royal Navy at the time Austen writing, nor has there ever been. However, the name is not entirely fanciful. "Laconia" was a region in ancient Greece

Jane Austen and the Military

where the city of Sparta was located. Classical names were popular in the Royal Navy at this time with the names of Greek and Roman gods or heroes being often used.

More to the point, a person who lived in ancient Laconia was known to the Greeks as a Lacedaemonian. And the was an HMS Lacedaemonian in service when Persuasion was first published. She was a Fifth Rate frigate, launched in 1812 and used in the North Atlantic to escort convoys to and from the Americas. Her biggest convoy was in 1813 when she, along with other Royal Navy ships, escorted no less than 550 merchant ships from Bermuda to Gibraltar. This ship may have served as a model for Austen's Laconia. She had a similar name, was of a similar type and served in the Atlantic.

In the Royal Navy at this date there were only two types of craft, despite the bewildering plethora of names and designations such as sloop, brig, frigate, cutter, corvette, schooner, lighter, hoy and all the rest. So far as the Admiralty was concerned there were really only ships and everything else. This division had important repercussions in a huge variety of ways. For a start ships were commanded by captains, all other vessels were commanded by lieutenants or commanders.

The difference in rank was clear, precise and of great importance. Lieutenants and commanders would be promoted only if the Admiralty felt they deserved it and if there was an opening into which they could be promoted. But once a man had reached the exalted rank of captain he was made for life.

Strictly speaking, the rank in the Royal Navy of Austen's time was "Post Captain". The term Post Captain was used to distinguish those who actually held the rank of Captain in the Royal Navy from those who were referred to as "captain" by virtue of commanding a ship be they a junior rank in the Royal Navy or in the merchant marine.

The name came from the fact that when an officer was promoted to this exalted rank a notice to this effect was "posted" into the London Gazette. This weekly newspaper is the official journal of the British

Jane Austen and the Military

Jane Austen and the Military

government which carries all the formal announcements of government appointments, actions and proclamations. The announcement of military promotions are just one of the many functions that this newspaper has served since it was first published in 1665.

The ships in the Royal Navy were first categorised into different sizes and ranks of importance in 1603. Unsurprisingly the system changed over time and by the Napoleonic Wars there were six "Rates" of warship. The most recent change to the system had come in 1801, but this was really only a minor tinkering with the Rating System of 1782. Basically the Rate assigned to a ship depended on the number of its guns, and from that much flowed.

A First Rate ship had 100 or more guns arranged on three decks that ran flat the entire length of the ship. There were other decks, of course, both below the water line and above the gun decks at the front and rear of the ship, but these were not counted. The guns carried by a First Rate were the largest taken to sea. On the lower gun deck were 42 pounders, the middle deck had 24 pounders and the upper deck 12 pounders. The weight of metal that a broadside from a First Rate could deliver was considered to be the pinnacle of maritime fighting. At this date the French were building bigger First Rates than the British - theirs mounted 120 or even 130 guns.

A Second Rate ship was, superficially, not much different from a First Rate. It too had three decks of guns and could carry between 90 and 100 guns. However, the guns were smaller. The lower gun deck carried 32 pounders, the middle deck 18 pounders and the upper deck 9 pounders. These lighter guns allowed the ships to be built smaller than the First Rates. A typical Second Rate was about 165 feet long

Facing page: HMS Victory, a First Rate, photographed in 1900 before she was moved into dry dock for preservation. She has three decks of guns, with lower deck mounting 42 pounders, the heaviest guns at sea at this date.

Jane Austen and the Military

on the gun deck, compared to 186 feet for a First Rate, and 45 feet wide, compared to 52 feet.

These differences in size and guns made a Second Rate considerably cheaper than a First Rate. That price difference was all the greater due to the fact that First Rates were recognised as being prestige ships. When a monarch went abroad, he went on a First Rate. That necessitated the inclusion of cabins of a size and opulence suitable for a royal passenger. The figurehead and other carvings that adorned a First Rate were commensurately lavish and ornate - and

HMS Ajax, a 74 gun Third Rate ship. These ships were the mainstay of the Royal Navy at this time. They were big enough to take part in the great battles between fleets, but small enough to be manoeuvrable in coastal waters and were cheaper to build than the bigger three decked First Rates and Second Rates.

Jane Austen and the Military

costly.

There was a lively debate in naval circles at the time Austen was writing as to which ship was the more potent weapon. First Rates could throw a heavier weight of metal in a more devastating broadside, but the big guns took longer to reload and the big ship was clumsier in light winds. The Second Rate fired less powerful guns, but could fire them more quickly and the ship was more nimble in its movements.

The true workhorse of most navies was, however, the Third Rate. These ships were of 64 to 80 guns, with the Royal Navy preferring a more or less standardised design that mounted 74 guns - they were known widely as "Seventy-Fours". These ships had two gun decks, with 24 pounders on the lower and 12 pounders on the upper decks. In size they were smaller than a Second Rate, being around 150 feet by 44 feet on the gun deck. The importance of the Seventy Fours can be seen from the numbers at sea. In 1814 there were 7 First Rates, 8 Second Rates and 103 Third Rates.

The First, Second and Third Rate warships were reckoned to be "ships of the line". This means that they were fit to fight in major battles, facing up against the big warships of the enemy. The usual formation in a major battle was for the ships to get into a line, one in front of the other, hence the term.

Smaller still than Third Rates for the Fourth Rates. These ships mounted 50 guns on two decks, with 18 pounders on the lower deck and 9 pounders on the upper. These were the smallest ships to have passenger quarters in what was known as the "coach", a suite of rooms tucked under the quarter deck at the rear of the ship. These were ideal for the use of an admiral. As a consequence most of the Fourth Rates were used as flagships in smaller fleets or in distant command stations such as the East Indies. In 1814 there were only ten such ships at sea.

Next came the Fifth Rates with between 32 and 44 guns. There was a single gun deck, carrying 12 pounders, though additional 9 pounder guns were mounted on the quarterdeck. These ships were

Jane Austen and the Military

typically around 136 feet long and 36 feet wide on the gun deck. The light size and armament made these ships fast, nimble and cheap, though they still fired a heavy enough broadside to be a potent threat to any merchant ship.

This design was, in fact, copied from the French who had begun making ships of this type in around 1735. The British began building them in 1757. The name was taken from a Spanish type of ship, the fragata, which was a light coastal craft.

Finally came the Sixth Rates, which were effectively smaller frigates mounting 24 guns of 18 and 9 pounder size. These were up to 110 feet long on the gun deck and 30 feet wide. A fair number of these smaller frigates were equipped with oars with which they could work in and out of small ports or coastal inlets even when the wind was against them. In 1814 there were 134 larger frigates and 25 of the smaller variety.

By putting Wentworth and Benwick into a frigate as a way of making them rich in a short period of time, Austen was absolutely correct. The frigates were designed to attack and to defend merchant ships. They took little or no part in major battles, but instead roved the seas hunting down enemy merchantmen. The capture of enemy commerce would weaken the enemy, but would make the crews and officers of the frigates rich indeed.

Chapter 9
The Enigma of Admiral Croft
(Persuasion)

Admiral Croft is something of an enigma. Much about him is left unsaid or unexplained. We are introduced to the Admiral in Chapter 3 when Mr Shepherd, the lawyer, is talking to Sir Walter Elliot about possible tenants for Kellynch Hall. Jane Austen describes Admiral Croft in some detail long before we meet him.

"It seemed as if Mr Shepherd, in this anxiety to bespeak Sir Walter's good will towards a naval officer as tenant, had been gifted with foresight; for the very first application for the house was from an Admiral Croft, with whom he shortly afterwards fell into company in attending the quarter sessions at Taunton; and indeed, he had received a hint of the Admiral from a London correspondent. By the report which he hastened over to Kellynch to make, Admiral Croft was a native of Somersetshire, who having acquired a very handsome fortune, was wishing to settle in his own country, and had come down to Taunton in order to look at some advertised places in that immediate neighbourhood, which, however, had not suited him; that accidentally hearing--(it was just as he had foretold, Mr *"Shepherd observed, Sir Walter's concerns could not be kept a secret,)--accidentally hearing of the possibility of Kellynch Hall being to let, and understanding his (Mr Shepherd's) connection with the owner, he had introduced himself to him in order to make particular inquiries, and had, in the course of a pretty long conference, expressed as strong an inclination for the*

Jane Austen and the Military

place as a man who knew it only by description could feel; and given Mr Shepherd, in his explicit account of himself, every proof of his being a most responsible, eligible tenant.

"And who is Admiral Croft?" was Sir Walter's cold suspicious inquiry.

Mr Shepherd answered for his being of a gentleman's family, and mentioned a place; and Anne, after the little pause which followed, added--

"He is a rear admiral of the white. He was in the Trafalgar action, and has been in the East Indies since; he was stationed there, I believe, several years."

"Then I take it for granted," observed Sir Walter, "that his face is about as orange as the cuffs and capes of my livery."

Mr Shepherd hastened to assure him, that Admiral Croft was a very hale, hearty, well-looking man, a little weather-beaten, to be sure, but not much, and quite the gentleman in all his notions and behaviour; not likely to make the smallest difficulty about terms, only wanted a comfortable home, and to get into it as soon as possible; knew he must pay for his convenience; knew what rent a ready-furnished house of that consequence might fetch; should not have been surprised if Sir Walter had asked more; had inquired about the manor; would be glad of the deputation, certainly, but made no great point of it; said he sometimes took out a gun, but never killed; quite the gentleman.

Mr Shepherd was eloquent on the subject; pointing out all the circumstances of the Admiral's family, which made him peculiarly desirable as a tenant. He was a married man, and without children; the "He was a married man, and without children; the very state to be wished for. A house was never taken good care of, Mr Shepherd observed, without a lady: he did not know, whether furniture might not be in danger of suffering as much where there was no lady, as where there were

Jane Austen and the Military

many children. A lady, without a family, was the very best preserver of furniture in the world. He had seen Mrs Croft, too; she was at Taunton with the admiral, and had been present almost all the time they were talking the matter over.

"And a very well-spoken, genteel, shrewd lady, she seemed to be," continued he; "asked more questions about the house, and terms, and taxes, than the Admiral himself, and seemed more conversant with business; and moreover, Sir Walter, I found she was not quite unconnected in this country, any more than her husband; that is to say, she is sister to a gentleman who did live amongst us once; she told me so herself: sister to the gentleman who lived a few years back at Monkford."

From this we know a number of things about Admiral Croft's career. Let us start with his rank as it is given when he is looking to rent Kellynch Hall. He holds the rank of Rear Admiral of the White. As admirals go, this is pretty low down the pecking order.

At the time Austen was writing there were ten ranks of Admiral in the Royal Navy. The most senior officer of all was the Admiral of the Fleet, of whom there was only one. The other nine ranks were arranged in a somewhat confusing order.

The more senior rank was Admiral. This title was derived from the term used for a senior naval officer by the Moslems of the Eastern Mediterranean, Amir-al-bahr. The term was adopted by the Venetians and other Christian states, becoming corrupted into variations of "admiral" as it did so. Originally an Admiral in English usage was the officer in charge of a fleet. The word became a definite rank within the Royal Navy by the 1610s.

As the Royal Navy became larger some way of distinguishing between senior and junior admirals arose. By the 1640s the ranks of Vice Admiral and Rear Admiral had been created. At this date - and until well into the 19th century - the conventional way to draw up a fleet of warships for battle was in a line with ships following each other. The fleet commander usually positioned himself in the centre.

Jane Austen and the Military

That meant that signal flags run up the masts of his flagship would be seen by as much of his fleet as possible even once the smoke of guns began to billow and obscure the view.

That battle smoke could, at times, become dense and it was not at all unusual for the ships at either end of the line of battle to be unable to see the signals from the flagship. It thus became usual for the most trustworthy captains to have their ships stationed as the first and last in the line. The position at the front was the more important since decisions taken there would have an impact on the ships following on behind.

When looking for subsidiary ranks, that of Vice Admiral was used to designate a flag officer senior enough to command the first ship in a line of battle. The rank of Rear Admiral was used to indicate an officer capable of commanding the rearmost ship. Thus the three main ranks of Admiral were, in descending order: Admiral, Vice Admiral and Rear Admiral.

However, the Royal Navy was also divided into three separate squadrons. Back in the 16th century these had been real squadrons of ships, but by Austen's time it was merely a convenient way of subdividing ships and officers. The Red Squadron took precedence over the White Squadron which was in turn more important than the Blue Squadron. Within each squadron an officer could have the rank of Admiral, Vice Admiral or Rear Admiral. So the path of promotion for admirals in the Royal Navy was to start as Rear Admiral of the Blue, then progress to Rear Admiral of the White before moving on in turn to be Rear Admiral of the White, Vice Admiral of the Blue, Vice Admiral of the White, Vice Admiral of the Red, Admiral of the Blue, Admiral of the White, Admiral of the Red and finally Admiral.

As a Rear Admiral of the White, therefore, Croft was on only the second of ten rungs in the promotion ladder for admirals. The rank held was, incidentally, no reflection at all on the competence or otherwise of the man in question. Once he was an admiral promotion came in strict order of seniority. When one admiral died or retired,

Jane Austen and the Military

the next below him would be promoted up to fill his rank, creating a vacancy for the next man down and so forth.

As can be imagined, this system could create a bit of a log jam in the senior ranks. The Admiralty therefore introduced a system nicknamed "Yellow Admirals". This involved offering an officer an immediate promotion up one rank on condition that they immediately retired. Older officers with younger men ahead of them were tempted by this and many took their pensions sooner than they might otherwise have done. Others were similarly promoted on the understanding that they were to take non-active positions such as being put in charge of a port or holding an administrative post at the Admiralty.

Admiral Horatio Nelson resplendent in his admiral's uniform and sporting some of the many decorations that he was awarded during his career at sea.

Jane Austen and the Military

If promotion was automatic, the holding of posts was not. It was entirely at the discretion of the Admiralty if an admiral held a command or not. Only the more capable officers would get an active command at sea. The fact that Croft "has been in the East Indies since; he was stationed there, I believe, several years" would mean that he was well regarded at the Admiralty. The East Indies was not the most sought after command, but it was nevertheless an active command.

At this date the East Indies trade was largely in the hands of the Dutch, the British concentrating more on India. Nevertheless, British merchant ships did trade very profitably with China and what is now Indonesia. And the growing colonies in Australia were becoming increasingly important as well. Pirates abounded in the eastern seas, as did frequent wars between the various petty states of the region. Keeping British merchant ships safe was a demanding task, so for Admiral Croft to have held a command in these waters for some years was a testament to his skills.

So far so good, Croft's naval career would appear to have been steady and successful if somewhat unspectacular. One small puzzle does occur when Anne remarks in passing that "He was in the Trafalgar action". This is the one and only time that Trafalgar is mentioned, although it was the most important naval battle of the era and gained even more importance from the fact that the great Admiral Nelson was killed there.

The battle was fought on 21 October 1805 off Cape Trafalgar in southern Spain. Nelson with 27 ships of the line faced the French Admiral Villeneuve with 33 French and Spanish ships of the line. After a long days fighting the Franco-Spanish fleet had been virtually destroyed. In all 21 Franco-Spanish ships had been captured and one sunk, with no loss in ships to the British. The victory saved Britain from a French invasion and, arguably, made an eventual British triumph over France merely a matter of time.

One key British casualty was, however, Nelson himself. His loss was an immense blow to the Royal Navy, but even more so to the

Jane Austen and the Military

British public. Nelson had achieved celebrity status akin to that of a modern film star through his repeated and spectacular naval victories over the French, combined with dashing good looks and a tempestuous personal life. He was undoubtedly the most charismatic naval officer since Drake two centuries earlier and was a great hero.

It is, therefore, rather odd that throughout the rest of the novel nobody asks Croft about either Trafalgar or about Nelson. Both would have been subjects of huge interest to people in England at the time of Persuasion, so the omission is odd. It is usually thought that this is because Austen inserted the reference to Trafalgar late in the novel's composition in order to give Croft's rather dull previous career a touch of glamour. But there may be a more personal issue at play.

Jane Austen's brother Sir Francis Austen was, in 1805, Captain of HMS Canopus. This was a powerful 84-gun Third Rate ship of the line, which had been captured from the French at an early Nelson victory at the Battle of the Nile. Sir Francis was serving under Nelson, cruising off the coast of Spain. When Villeneuve initially came out, he slipped past Nelson and went to the West Indies to link up with other French ships. Nelson, with Sir Francis and the Canopus, followed only to arrive too late to catch Villeneuve who had made his rendezvous and returned to Spain.

Turning back across the Atlantic, Nelson found that the now combined enemy fleet had gone back into harbour. Thinking that the campaign was over, Nelson went back to Britain for a month's leave, then returned to his fleet. By the time he got there the ships were very low on supplies. Nelson therefore sent five ships - including the Canopus - to Gibraltar to escort back a convoy of merchant ships that was ready to sail with the supplies. Just days later, while Canopus and Sir Francis were absent, the great Battle of Trafalgar was fought. Thus Sir Francis Austen missed taking part in the greatest naval battle of British history by a matter of days and bad luck.

It may be that the subject of Trafalgar was one that was tactfully avoided in the Austen household.

Jane Austen and the Military

Regarding Croft's career, if he were a Rear Admiral of the White in 1818 when Persuasion was published, he would have almost certainly been a captain of a ship of the line in 1805. Needless to say there was no Captain Croft in command of one of Nelson's ships at Trafalgar. Nor does Austen actually say that he was in command of a ship at Trafalgar merely that "He was in the Trafalgar action".

It is all rather odd.

Another slightly puzzling aspect of Croft's naval career is revealed in a conversation between Mrs Musgrove and Mrs Croft in Chapter 8. Mrs Musgrove remarks that as a naval wife, Mrs Croft must have travelled a good deal and turns to her for confirmation. Mrs Croft is the first speaker in this exchange:

"Pretty well, ma'am in the fifteen years of my marriage; though many women have done more. I have crossed the Atlantic four times, and have been once to the East Indies, and back again, and only once; besides being in different places about home: Cork, and Lisbon, and Gibraltar. But I never went beyond the Streights, and never was in the West Indies. We do not call Bermuda or Bahama, you know, the West Indies."

Mrs Musgrove had not a word to say in dissent; she could not accuse herself of having ever called them anything in the whole course of her life.

"And I do assure you, ma'am," pursued Mrs Croft, *"that nothing can exceed the accommodations of a man-of-war; I speak, you know, of the higher rates. When you come to a frigate, of course, you are more confined; though any reasonable woman may be perfectly happy in one of them; and I can safely say, that the happiest part of my life has been spent on board a ship. While we were together, you know, there was nothing to be feared. Thank God! I have always been blessed with excellent health, and no climate disagrees with me. A little disordered always the first twenty-four hours of going to sea, but never knew what sickness was afterwards. The only time I*

Jane Austen and the Military

ever really suffered in body or mind, the only time that I ever fancied myself unwell, or had any ideas of danger, was the winter that I passed by myself at Deal, when the Admiral (Captain Croft then) was in the North Seas. I lived in perpetual fright at that time, and had all manner of imaginary complaints from not knowing what to do with myself, or when I should hear from him next; but as long as we could be together, nothing ever ailed me, and I never met with the smallest inconvenience."

It can be concluded from this that Mrs Croft accompanied her husband in his naval voyages - except early in their marriage when she was left at Deal. She specifically remarks "that nothing can exceed" the Admiral's quarters on board a ship of the line.

However, during the years that Croft was an active sea officer Britain was almost constantly at war. It was extremely unusual for a serving naval officer to take his wife with him to sea - indeed almost unheard of. Whatever Mrs Croft might say on the subject, quarters in a warship were always rather cramped and privacy was all but impossible.

It was, of course, more normal for wives to accompany admirals and captains when they were stationed to far flung parts of the world - as when Croft was sent to the East Indies. But when this was the case, the wives sailed out in merchant convoys where the dangers were fewer and the comforts greater.

It is likely that in creating Mrs Croft and her rather unorthodox career, Jane Austen was drawing on her real life sister in law, Fanny the wife of Charles Austen. Captain Charles Austen met and fell in love with the 15 year old Fanny on Bermuda, where her father was Attorney General. Soon after their marriage in 1807, Charles was transferred to Halifax, Nova Scotia, and he took his new wife with him on board his ship. When Charles was moved back to Europe, he again took his wife with him on board his ship. Almost certainly Mrs Croft's travels on board her husband's ships are based on those of

Jane Austen and the Military

Fanny Austen. Presumably Jane Austen mistook the rather unusual exploits of her sister in law for what was normal.

The Battle of Trafalgar by William Clarkson Stanfield. The close range at which naval battles were fought at this date is shown clearly in this painting.

Chapter 10
Conclusion

Looking at the way Jane Austen writes about the military in her novels, it is striking how accurate she is - but also the way that a few errors stand out. On the whole, she gets most of her details correct. This can come as little surprise. For most of her life Britain was at war and for some years that war posed a very real threat of invasion by a French army that was not known for its gentle treatment of civilians.

The military would, therefore, have been a more or less constant presence in Jane Austen's life. Even without her brothers in the navy, a young woman living in Hampshire would have been familiar with army and militia regiments marching to and fro, coastal defences manned by soldiers and naval ships putting in and our of nearby harbours.

Just as during more recent conflicts, the exploits of the military filled the pages of the newspapers and were the topic of conversation and gossip across the land. Jane Austen was clearly an observant and attentive person for she picked up much about the exclusively male world of the military and entwined what she learned into her works. Indeed, by featuring military men as often as she did, Austen was accurately reflecting the society in which she moved.

When Austen does make errors it is for understandable reasons. Colonel Brandon and Colonel Fitzwilliam are intended to be gentlemen of means with a military past. The rank of colonel was precisely right for the types of character that Austen wanted them to be in her novels, and so she ascribed them this rank. That this may

Jane Austen and the Military

have caused some minor inconsistencies with their back-stories was not really Austen's concern.

She makes only two real errors. The first is one of omission; she does not mention that young William Price had to pass a stringent and difficult exam to be made up to lieutenant in the Royal Navy. Instead she rather implies that his promotion is down to influence and patronage. However, it is the patronage that is key to the developing plot and relationships between the characters in the novel. Young William's ability to pass an exam may have been crucial to him, but is entirely irrelevant to the novel.

Rather more serious is the way she puts a youthful Colonel Brandon in the East Indies at a date when no British troops were stationed there at all. There is no way around this. It is an error, pure and simple.

But if that is the sole error that Jane Austen makes when writing of the military then she has done better than many other novelists. We really have nothing very much to complain about at all.

Jane Austen and the Military

Jane Austen and the Military

About the Author

Rupert Matthews is an historian and author of non-fiction books, magazine articles and newspaper columns. His work has been translated into 28 languages (including Sioux).

Rupert has appeared on television and radio for over 20 years as presenter, interviewer and expert witness. He has an authoritative presence that works well on screen whether he is acting as expert witness or presenter. He has the knack of being able to impart historical information in an engaging manner, allowing even complex information to be accessible to the general public.

As well as appearing on screen, Rupert has acted as consultant to a number of television, theatre and movie projects to ensure historical accuracy.